Materials

and Interior Design

Published in 2012
by Laurence King Publishing Ltd
361–373 City Road
London EC1V 1LR
Tel +44 20 7841 6900
Fax +44 20 7841 6910
E enquiries@laurenceking.com
www.laurenceking.com

A catalog record for this book is available from the British Library

ISBN 978 1 85669 759 0
Designed by John Round Design
Printed in China

Materials
and Interior Design

Rachael Brown and Lorraine Farrelly

Laurence King Publishing

Contents

Related study material is available on the Laurence King website at
www.laurenceking.com

Introduction

Until very recently, there has been a limited range of reference books that document the history and practice of interior design as a specific activity, and there has been a scarcity of relevant texts to promote critical thinking in interior design. However, a more complete and inclusive history is beginning to emerge and interior design texts, readers, and guides are being introduced by new authors and educators who are informing contemporary practice. We have drawn upon these references, and it is hoped that this book makes its own contribution, particularly as a resource for the design student who is seeking to learn more about the use of materials in the interior design context.

Understanding how materials are selected, composed, and assembled is an essential skill for interior design. Designers must be able to assess the aesthetic and functional properties of materials while maintaining an ethical,

investigative, and innovative approach to design. They must also understand how their choice of materials will define the character of an interior environment and inform how the space is experienced by its occupants.

This book aims to explore these themes: the relationship between materials and the interior environment. It examines how and why materials are selected for different contexts, the "readings" and meanings of materials, how materials are assembled and applied, how the designer's material concepts and intentions are represented and communicated at various stages of a project, and the sources that designers can use when selecting materials, material types, and methodologies for classifying materials. The book also includes case studies that exemplify different uses of materials in the interior.

The book is organized under the following principal headings:

Part I. Historical context of materials and interior design

How materials are used in an interior environment can be informed by historical, cultural, and physical contexts, and the traditions and conventions that the designer absorbs. Traditional uses of materials and construction processes will vary according to time and place; established practices can be adopted or adapted by designers, and these methods may be combined with, or replaced by, contemporary technologies and materials. When selecting and assembling materials, designers might also draw inspiration from other cultural practices of their society or the wider, global community of artists and designers, such as painters, sculptors, fashion designers, and furniture designers.

This section introduces some of the influences that informed the use of materials in interior design during the nineteenth and twentieth centuries.

Opposite
"étapes" exhibition at Villa Noailles, Hyères, France, 2008. The exhibition included three products by the Bouroullec brothers: Raintiles, a fabric tile with integral connectors, designed for Kvadrat (left); Algues, designed for Vitra (top right); and Roc, a prototype room definer/divider also designed for Vitra using fabric-covered cardboard components (bottom right).

Above left and right
The Castelvecchio Museum, Verona (left) and Querini-Stampalia Foundation, Venice (right), exemplify Carlo Scarpa's mastery of the selection and juxtaposition of materials in historic building projects.

Part II. Selection

When considering materials for an interior at the initial stages of a project, the designer will need to engage with the client, the brief, and the site. As part of this briefing process, key design issues and considerations such as the client's visual identity, values, functional aspirations, and spatial needs; cost; program; and issues concerning sustainability will be discussed and defined. This analytical process of engagement will also include a "reading" of the site—this may be an existing site, one that exists only in the form of drawings and models, or an imagined locale yet to be identified.

These initial discussions generally result in a more clearly defined brief and an understanding of opportunities and limitations: the creative parameters within which designers will generate their ideas and select materials. At this point, design concepts may begin to emerge and will be presented using precedent images or reference projects, material samples, and experimental sketches and models. Discussions and debates will ensue, alternatives will be tested and the refinements of the concept progressed until a clear design proposal is identified and agreed.

During this process, a palette of materials will be considered: materials of both the existing site and those of the interior intervention. These materials may be the generators for the concept and form-making or may be assembled as a response to the spatial concepts (i.e. form follows materials or materials follow form). Designers may draw their inspiration for using materials directly from the site and the project brief, or they may look beyond these starting points to the work of other practitioners operating in a wide range of disciplines.

Above

Papercut, Yeshop Inhouse showroom, Athens, by dARCHstudio. In some cases the choice of main material is a generator of the project, and in other cases the choice of material is a response to the site or the brief.

Above right

Ruth Morrow and Trish Belford's product "Girli Concrete" (a concrete and textile tile) exemplifies how conventions can be challenged and how different materials can be juxtaposed.

Above

Consideration of a material's color and texture is a vital part of concept development. Designers will often begin by gathering together samples (in this case for carpet).

Part III. Application

Once design concepts have been proposed and agreed upon, the designer will begin a rigorous process of assessing the materials palette and the various aesthetic and functional properties of the materials selected. This will include issues of composition, durability, and sustainability.

The materials that are finally selected will be specified to create a cohesive whole, a specific atmosphere, and a "balanced" relationship of functional and sensory properties. Subtle changes or adjustments to any of the ingredients could change the reading of the interior environment.

In addition to the overall palette, the designer will also consider how materials will be juxtaposed and assembled: the detail of joints, junctions, fixings, and fastenings (often the generator for design concepts, a starting point rather than the end of the process).

Top
Finely detailed junctions between marble elements at Scarpa's Castelvecchio, Verona.

Above
"Camper Together," 2009, Paris and Copenhagen, by Studio Bouroullec. In this retail interior the designers have considered the composition of complementary colors and contrasting textures.

Part IV. Communicating from concept to completion

The process of recording observations, thinking through drawing, and developing concepts and design proposals for the use and application of materials in interiors can be represented and communicated in many ways by the designer. Some methods, such as sketching, form part of the designer's personal journey and inquiry of design, while other methods are used to communicate intentions to a wide group of people, including the client, the occupants, the contractor, and the installer.

When communicating the visual quality of an interior and the properties of the materials selected, drawings such as freehand sketches, measured perspectives, and axonometrics may be used. Designers will also use models, computer-generated images and animations, and material samples.

To accompany these often seductive visual images and artifacts, more precise plans and sections are required to locate the material in context. Technical detail drawings are also completed to describe how the materials are to be assembled and constructed.

At the construction stage of a project, materials may also need to be described in writing. This written documentation is usually referred to as a specification: a list of materials that will be used in a space and a description of the sources or suppliers, how the materials will be finished and assembled, and any special issues that need to be addressed.

Left
A freehand perspective drawing is often the most effective way to communicate an early concept to a client. This example illustrates the Sportsmuseum, Flevohof, the Netherlands, by Rem Koolhaas and Luc Reuse (OMA).

Below
A computer-generated visualization for a sports venue.

Part V. Material classifications and sources

Materials can be grouped and described using a number of different approaches. They might be classified according to their constituent parts, i.e. natural, synthetic, composite, etc.; or according to their possible applications or functional requirements, i.e. walls, floors, ceilings, etc. There are many other methods of archiving and classifying materials, such as scientific, sensory, or aesthetic groupings, which can challenge the designer's conventional practice. Different material types are also manufactured and finished using a range of traditional and contemporary processes.

There is a vast range of manufacturers and suppliers who can provide information and samples of materials that designers might collect in their practice library. In addition, designers have access to established archives and libraries of materials—physical, in books and online—that can provide inspiration and suggest alternative uses and applications of those materials.

Such libraries and archives can often unite the scientific production of materials with the innovative designer looking for new possibilities and solutions.

Part VI. Case studies

A number of case studies have been identified in order to exemplify particular uses of materials, for example: how materials are used to communicate a client's brand, values, and identity; sustainable approaches to using materials; methods of construction; an artist's approach to materials in interior design; interdisciplinary approaches to using materials in interiors; and creating atmospheres through the selection of materials.

This page
A selection of various materials.

Woven plastic

Mother-of-pearl mosaic

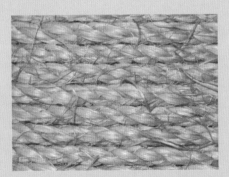
Natural seagrass flooring

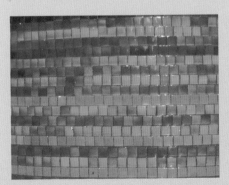
Glass mosaic

Marble

PART I HISTORICAL CONTEXT OF MATERIALS AND INTERIOR DESIGN

Now is an exciting time to practice interior design. Owing to environmental and economic pressures, buildings are frequently being reused rather than rebuilt and interior designers are recognized as having the skills to make a sensitive intervention within an existing interior. In addition, design studios often have an interdisciplinary approach to design whereby interior designers, graphic designers, product and furniture designers, textile designers, artists, and architects work collaboratively on projects: interior designers work on graphics, architects detail products, and textile designers and artists work spatially. This interdisciplinary approach to design allows boundaries to be crossed and methodologies to be transferred, producing fertile working environments and innovative design solutions. This is particularly relevant when considering how materials are used in an interior.

Alongside these shifts in working practices, new technologies have transformed design and manufacturing processes, producing a new generation of sophisticated materials that the innovative designer can combine with more traditional methods to create inspiring contemporary interiors.

All designers are influenced by the particular time and place in which they practice; design concepts are conceived and executed within a particular cultural context and are informed by the opportunities and constraints of society. Traditions of design are inherited, absorbed, and adapted to respond to contemporary environments and users' needs. Design can be reactive to taste and informed by a range of social and cultural influences, from economics, politics, and technology to film, literature, fashion, and textiles to art and architecture. Designers are also influenced by their predecessors, who have provided a rich seam of inspiration and knowledge to be mined by successive generations.

In this section of the book we shall examine how historically, some of these issues have influenced the selection of materials for interior applications, and we will identify some of the key individuals who are recognized as having had a significant influence on the design of interiors.

Below and below right
"Ideal House" exhibition
2004, Cologne, Germany,
by Studio Bouroullec. In this
installation, Studio Bouroullec
use polymeric, injection-
molded components (called
"Algues") which are connected
to create a division of space.

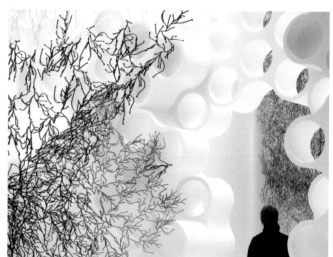

1. The Industrial Age: Design movements and their materials

The Industrial Revolution in Europe and America transformed methods of production and the use of materials in product, furniture, and interior design. Manufacturing processes became increasingly mechanized, coal-fueled steam power was adopted (replacing water mills, humans, and animals as the primary source of power) and transportation improved, giving industries access to a plentiful supply of minerals and raw materials. These changes were particularly significant for iron and steel production and also the textiles industry, which increased its capacity to produce a diverse range of fabrics for different applications; the quest for wholly man-made materials (synthetics) can also be traced back to this period.

The Industrial Revolution led to a shift away from the handcrafted product to mass-produced goods such as ceramics, furniture, carpets, and other domestic objects. The production of wallpapers and textiles for curtains and upholstery, formerly hand block-printed, was transformed by mechanization and the invention of cheap aniline dyes[1], which replaced the natural pigments extracted from insects, leaves, and flowers. These changes allowed wallpapers and textiles to be produced in abundance and in a kaleidoscope of colors and patterns.

During this period standards of living were rising and the middle-class consumer emerged with the income to invest in the design of their domestic interiors, following fashionable trends and often adopting a style that emulated the homes of their social superiors.[2] Items that had previously been regarded as luxurious were viewed as necessities, and an era of mass consumerism and the quest for instant gratification began. The populace was enthralled by the novelty of abundance,[3] and industry now had the potential to deliver good and affordable design to a mass market.

Another significant change triggered by the Industrial Revolution was artificial lighting. In the age of candlelight and gaslight (introduced into homes in the Victorian era) dark materials were selected to mask the dirty marks left by flames, and reflective materials, gilt, and mirrors were used in interiors to enhance the effect of the lighting. By the end of the Victorian period, electric light was used in many homes and this changed the functionality and aesthetic qualities of some of the materials selected.

1 Deborah Cohen, *Household Gods, the British and their Possessions*, New Haven: Yale University Press, 2006, p. 36.
2 Anne Massey, *Interior Design since 1900*, London: Thames & Hudson, 2008, p. 7.
3 Cohen, op cit., p. 34.

Below
The Tea, oil on canvas, c.1880, by Mary Cassatt. A depiction of a middle-class interior furnished with the products of the Industrial Revolution: mass-produced textiles, wallpapers, crockery, and silverware. (Photograph ©2012 Museum of Fine Arts, Boston.)

Below left
William Morris' preference for the handcrafted is evident in his own home, Kelmscott Manor, Gloucestershire, England.

Below right
The dark stained wood used in Charles Rennie Mackintosh's Glasgow School of Art, Scotland, has a handcrafted quality.

Not all designers and commentators of the period embraced these changes. John Ruskin (1819–1900), a very influential artist, poet, and critic, lamented the shift away from craft production and considered it to be dehumanizing and immoral:

It was Ruskin's bitter denunciation of the design of industrially produced objects that impacted most strongly on the Arts and Crafts movement. The assumption that machine-made things would inevitably be tasteless and garish led to advocacy of a return to hand craft as the only possible route to reform.[4]

The Arts and Crafts Movement was founded by William Morris (1834–1896) a writer, designer, and socialist. He believed in the intrinsic value of handmade products, which, unlike mass-produced artifacts, are imbued with the mark and mind of their maker. He established Morris, Marshall, Faulkner & Co. with partners including Edward Burne-Jones and Dante Gabriel Rossetti; this company became Morris & Co., makers of hand-printed textiles and wallpaper that are still available today. The handcrafted approach to the use of materials can be seen in the design of Morris' own home, Kelmscott Manor: hand-printed wallpaper; richly colored and decorative handmade rugs as wall hangings—the mark of the carpenter, the metalworker, and the upholsterer are all visible. Stylistically and philosophically, the Arts and Crafts Movement had much in common with the Gothic Revivalists, including a tendency to look back to and romanticize the past.

4 John Pile, *A History of Interior Design*, London: Laurence King, 2000, p. 267.

Charles Rennie Mackintosh (1868–1928) was a Scottish architect and designer known for his architecture, interiors, and furniture designs. He inherited some of the traditions of the Arts and Crafts Movement, evident in his highly crafted use of materials in projects such as Hill House in Helensburgh, 1902, and the Glasgow School of Art, 1907–9. However, having traveled in Europe he was also influenced by and was a proponent of the Continental art and design movement, Art Nouveau, which grew in the 1890s.

Art Nouveau advocated an interdisciplinary approach to design, with artists, designers, and architects working collaboratively on fully integrated interiors and architecture (an approach that can be observed in many design practices today). Its exponents embraced some of the changes brought about by the Industrial Revolution, particularly the production of new materials:

The progress made in iron construction during the second half of the nineteenth century is crucial for the development of the Art Nouveau interior. ... The early Art Nouveau's frank exposure of metal in the domestic interior had radical implications in the context of the traditional styles and materials used by Beaux-Arts architects.[5]

In 1862, at the London International Exhibition, European artists and designers were exposed to a significant collection of Japanese art and artifacts including lacquered woodwork, woodcuts, prints, and textiles. Although Japanese art and design had long since been influential in the West, this exhibition (and Japonisme in general) had a significant impact on the artists and designers of the period and also those of subsequent generations, such as Eileen Gray (1878–1976) and Aubrey Beardsley (1872–98). Beardsley's use of fluid line and composition clearly references the art of Japan, and in turn his work was inspirational to leading designers of the Art Nouveau movement—for example, Victor Horta in Belgium and his use of exposed, decorative metalwork and vegetal forms; and Hector Guimard in France, famous for his designs for the Paris Métro. The Art Nouveau designers used materials to create organic forms and highly decorative, patterned surfaces, rich in color and texture.

As well as being influenced by European design, Charles Rennie Mackintosh had a significant influence on the Vienna Secessionists. The Secessionists were keen to break away from established practices and traditions of art and architecture in Austria, and like the Art Nouveau designers they blurred "professional" boundaries and aimed to unite the arts: painting, design, architecture, and music. Like the practitioners of the Arts and Crafts Movement, they had a preference for good-quality handcrafted fixtures

5 Massey, op. cit, 2008, p. 33.

Below
The woodwork of the dining room at the Victor Horta Museum, Brussels, exemplifies the distinctive organic forms of Art Nouveau.

Bottom
Hector Guimard used decorative ironwork and glass to create the distinctive vegetal entrances to the Paris Métro.

Below left
Architects, artists, and designers collaborated on the design for the XIV Secessionist Exhibition interior, Vienna, 1902. Gustav Klimt's frieze, which was painted directly onto the walls, can be seen in the background.

Bottom left
The use of materials in Eileen Gray's rue de Lota apartment in Paris bridged Art Deco, the Moderne, and Modernism. This image shows the apartment after a refurbishment in 1930 by Paul Ruaud; her Pirogue Chaise can be seen on the left.

Below right
A designer of furniture and interiors, Emile-Jacques Ruhlmann was influenced by Art Nouveau, the Arts and Crafts Movement, and eighteenth-century furniture. He used opulent materials, particularly rare woods, as illustrated in this 1926 watercolor of an interior.

and fittings, and artwork that was integrated in order to create holistic and decorative interiors.

In 1917, a period influenced by the emergence of the Modernist movement in architecture and Art Deco, Eileen Gray designed the interior for the rue de Lota apartment. She conceived all the interior elements—the rooms, the furniture, and the products—creating a hybrid of Modernist and decorative approaches to design. She furnished the apartment with her own products, including her Pirogue Chaise, Serpent Chair, and lacquered Block Screen (she had learned how to use Japanese lacquering techniques). Other items of furniture were also designed by Gray for this context, resulting in a cohesive "whole"; this interior, along with her other work, had a significant influence on her contemporaries and future generations of designers.

The Art Deco movement gained recognition in France in the 1920s, and grew to have an influence on international art and design—particularly in the UK and America. Art Deco referenced a diverse range of design influences, from African art, Aztec designs, and Egyptian art and design. In 1922 Howard Carter unearthed the tomb of Tutankhamen, and this gave a significant stimulus to the public's interest in Egyptian styling, a fashion

Right
In the Maison de Verre, Paris, France, Pierre Chareau juxtaposed materials used by Art Deco designers and the decorative arts with those made available by the Industrial Revolution and preferred by the Modernists.

Below right
Schröder House, Utrecht, the Netherlands, Gerrit Rietveld, 1924. The selection, form, and detailing of materials reflects Rietveld's background in furniture making, and also corresponds with De Stijl principles.

adopted by Art Deco designers: cinemas, factories such as the Hoover Building, and furniture were "Egyptianized." Opulent, rare, and ostentatious materials such as inlaid mahogany and ebony, real animal furs, and highly lacquered finishes were combined with more modern materials such as aluminum and Bakelite, the first mass-produced plastic.

The Deco style was interpreted for Hollywood film sets, for example in the designs of Cedric Gibbons for films such as *Grand Hotel* (1932) and *Born to Dance* (1936); Fritz Lang's *Metropolis* (1927); and Darrell Silvera's sets for *Swing Time* (1936). These glamorous films helped to internationalize and popularize the movement's style, use of materials and decoration, which was then adapted for ordinary, domestic interiors. During this period, a number of prominent women began to have a particularly pronounced influence on interior decoration and design, for example, Candace Wheeler, Edith Wharton, Elsie de Woolf, and Syrie Maugham—the last-named known for her white interior, designed for a villa in Le Touquet.

Another important figure in the history of interior design also working in this period was Pierre Chareau (1883–1950). Like Eileen Gray, his use of materials was also influenced by both Modernist principles and the decorative arts. In his design for the Maison de Verre (House of Glass, 1928–32) in Paris, France, he juxtaposes exposed structural steel beams, used to create a free plan (a plan without load-bearing partitions), with Art Deco furnishings; glazed elevations (using glass blocks) with decorative room dividers; and contemporary materials such as perforated metals, rubbers, and concrete with refined wooden furniture and fabrics.

A contemporary of Chareau, Gerrit Rietveld, was a member of the artistic movement De Stijl, and applied the philosophy of this movement to the design of

the Schröder House (1924), Utrecht, the Netherlands, which he designed in collaboration with the client, Mrs Truus Schröder-Schräder. The house is claimed to be an embodiment of De Stijl principles: the use of material forms; vertical and horizontal planes that slide and intersect; and furniture, primary colors and essential, "truthful" materials that appear as a three-dimensional interpretation of a Piet Mondrian painting. The materials used are simple, and were assembled using joinery techniques. It is important to note that the De Stijl movement influenced the founders of the Bauhaus in Germany (1919–33), including Modernist architect Walter Gropius, and that the Bauhaus in turn propelled Modernism and has influenced many generations of designers and educators.

Modernist architects and designers embraced the changes to manufacturing brought about by the

Industrial Revolution. They were inspired by systems of mass production, efficiency, and the standardization of components; by new materials such as concrete, mild steel, and expansive glass; and by developments in other fields of design, such as the automotive and aeronautical industries. They claimed to eschew applied decoration (a stance first advocated by Adolf Loos in *Ornament and Crime*, 1908), instead advocating a "truth to materials"[6] and a doctrine of "form ever follows function,"[7] wherein materials are used appropriately according to their functional properties and their essential qualities are revealed, precluding the need for decorative veneers, plastering, paint and "faux" materials (one material imitating another).

The use of structural steel and concrete meant that solid, loadbearing walls were no longer a necessity; this led to the liberation of the plan (the "free plan" as promoted by Swiss architect Le Corbusier as one of his five points of architecture) and the elevation. Inside and outside were no longer polarized as spatial experiences, as expansive use of glass led to fluid connections between the two: the exterior became the material landscape of the interior.

One of the visions of the Modernists was to create a utopian urban environment, an ideal that responded to modern industry, mechanization, science, and manufacturing and that ruptured connections with outmoded traditions of the past. The influence of this vision (although somewhat distorted) can be seen in the housing of the post-war era: low-budget, high-density high-rise flats with functional, compact interiors.

During World War II, the British Government introduced the Utility Scheme in response to a shortage of materials and labor. Furniture could only be purchased using a points system, and the prices of materials and furniture were fixed. The styling of the furniture adopted some Modernist conventions and use of material was minimized, resulting in a limited choice of products and a lean, minimal (in terms of scale and materials) approach to design. This utilitarian response corresponded with the aesthetic and scale of post-war social housing.

This approach to wartime domestic furnishing and post-war housing clearly illustrates the importance of wealth, labor, and availability of materials in the evolution of interiors—issues relevant to contemporary designers.

The Surrealist, Pop Art, and Op Art movements have also influenced the use of materials in interiors; this is particularly evident in the domestic and retail interiors of the 1960s and 1970s, in which the room became "an Environment, a Happening, or a Painting."[8] The principles and concepts of these movements corresponded with consumerist/Pop culture's disregard for tradition and longevity, and its hunger for new polymeric or disposable products which quickly become obsolete:

Pop design's challenge to notions about tradition and longevity was further emphasized by the production of disposable furniture. The lack of seriousness and playfulness of Pop created an atmosphere in which furniture could be made from sturdy card, assembled by the purchaser, enjoyed for a month or so and then, discarded as the next model appeared.[9]

6 A concept attributable to John Ruskin, and associated with the artist Henry Moore.
7 A phrase coined by US architect Louis Sullivan in 1896.
8 Massey, op. cit., p. 185.
9 Ibid., p. 178.

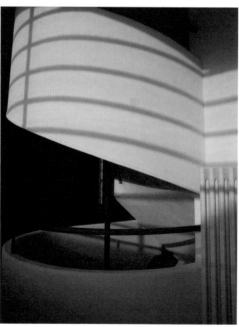

Far left and left
Barcelona Pavilion, by Ludwig Mies van der Rohe, 1928–9, and Villa Savoye, Poissy, by Le Corbusier, 1928–30. Le Corbusier and Mies responded positively to the new materials and technologies of the industrial era, and were leaders of the Modernist movement in architecture. In the Barcelona Pavilion, Mies created a free plan using glass and steel columns, which are set on a plinth of travertine; vertical planes of travertine and green and gold onyx are used to define the space. At the Villa Savoye, Le Corbusier used less opulent materials: concrete, ceramic and mosaic tiles, and glass.

Below
The influence of the Pop Art movement can be seen in Ben Kelly's interior for the Haçienda nightclub in Manchester, 1982. Set against a cool blue background, bright graphic imagery borrowed from the urban environment, catseyes and bollards (normally used for roads) are used to deliniate the interior, creating a city within a city.

Right
Ettore Sottsass and the Memphis Group had an eclectic, Postmodernist approach to materials, drawing influence from Pop Art, Op Art, Art Deco, and classical design. The Casablanca cabinet of 1981, pictured, makes reference to classical furniture but its decorative, plastic laminate finishes are a celebration of modern consumer culture.

In the latter part of the twentieth century economic booms continued to fuel the demand for retail, commercial, and domestic interiors, leading to the recognition of interior design as a practice in its own right. In this Postmodernist period there was no unifying rhetoric or ideology; however, the influence of preceding movements in design could be observed.

The Memphis Group, a movement founded in the 1980s by Italian designer Ettore Sottsass (1917–2007), embodied Postmodern ideologies. Designers such as Sottsass, American architect Michael Graves, and Austrian architect Hans Hollein eschewed the dogma of Modernism, drawing inspiration from Surrealism, Pop Art, and Op Art, using bold colors, patterned laminates, and elaborate forms; references to Art Deco can also be observed. The designs this group produced had a global influence.

French designer Philippe Starck (born 1949) and Dutch architect Rem Koolhaas (born 1944) were also working in this period. Starck designs both products and interiors and, like other Postmodernists, his work has referenced an eclectic range of genres and styles.

Rem Koolhaas is the founding partner of OMA. OMA's design for the Netherlands Dance Theater in The Hague (1987) applies a dynamic and unpredictable approach to the use of materials and form.

In contrast, the minimalists, also working in the 1980s, continued and adapted Modernist traditions; the inherent qualities of materials were utilized and revealed and designs were stripped back to the bare essentials:

With their overtones of a pared-down Japanese aesthetic, minimalist interiors of the 1980s and 1990s offered a highly publicized oasis of calm in both domestic and retail spaces that seemed to continue the Modernist tradition of imposing order and regulation upon their inhabitants.[10]

The late twentieth century also marked the beginnings of the Technological Revolution and the Information Age, sociological transformations that had their expression in architecture and design in a style known as High-Tech.

10 Sparke, Massey, Keeble et al, *Designing the Modern Interior*, Oxford: Berg, 2009, p. 221.

Below and below right
In OMA's design for the Netherlands Dance Theater, the materials used appear as disconnected fragments. Industrial materials such as folded sheet steel are juxtaposed and collaged with more expensive materials and finishes such as stucco, marble, and gold foil.

Richard Rogers' (British, born 1933) and Renzo Piano's (Italian, born 1937) iconic design for the Pompidou Center (1971–7) is a notable example. This was also an era where former industrial buildings and sites such as docklands, warehouses, and factories were beginning to be redeveloped.[11] These concurrent events produced an exciting hybrid: the original industrial materials of existing buildings were juxtaposed with new materials selected for their industrial aesthetic, and modern mechanical, electrical, and technological infrastructures were revealed. This High-Tech, industrial approach was still influential at the end of the century and can be observed in STUDIOS architecture's interior for the Cartoon Network in Burbank, California (completed 2000), and Future Systems' design for Comme des Garçons, New York (1998). The influence of technology was also changing material production, form-making, and construction processes, as discussed later in this chapter.

11 Ibid., p. 224.

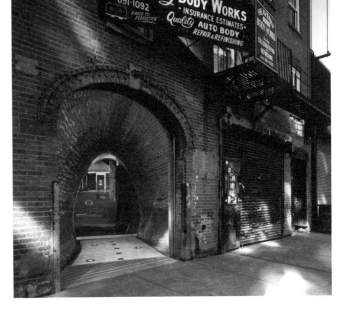

Top

John Pawson's interior for the fashion retailer Jigsaw exemplifies the minimalist approach to materials: the rich textural qualities of the clothing are contrasted with the cool, calm, pared-down interior of etched acrylic screens, stone, and white walls.

Above

St Martins Lane Hotel, London. Philippe Starck's playful designs are often an assembly of disparate elements and materials such as plastic, velvet, gold leaf, and glass, composed to create a theatrical tableau. Starck also manipulates familiar forms by changing their scale and context to create surreal compositions.

Above

Like the bell of a saxophone, Future Systems' brushed-aluminum, tubular entrance insertion creates a threshold that links interior and exterior, the old and the new. The tube is a monocoque structure formed from ¼ in sheets of aluminum with seamless joints; the door is a single sheet of glass with an offset pivot hinge.

2. The evolution of materials

One of the most significant technological developments that influenced interior design in the twentieth century was the production of plastics and their associated materials and products. These included Bakelite, the first synthetic mass-produced plastic; nylon, the first entirely man-made fiber; other synthetic polymers, such as PVC and polystyrene; molded plastics (plastic forms created using heat or pressure); and plastic laminates.

The world wars and the burgeoning automotive industries gave impetus to the research and development of materials and advanced technologies such as the injection molding of plastics and the forming and gluing of plywood;[12] these technologies informed the design of interiors, products, and furniture.

Furniture, or more specifically the chair, is often significant in defining the material quality of an interior, and, perhaps because of their scale (compared to rooms and buildings), chairs often serve as prototypes for new, evolving materials and manufacturing processes. Chairs often become iconic because they embody the material innovations of their era and go on to influence how materials are used in other contexts, such as the built environment. Notable examples include: Thonet's Chair No. 14 (1859), one of the first mass-produced chairs, made using steam to bend solid wood; Marcel Breuer's Wassily Chair (1920s), which pioneered and defined the use of seamless steel tubing; Charles and Ray Eames' Shell Chair (1952), the first to be mass produced in plastic, and also their "family" of molded plywood chairs, still manufactured by Vitra today; and Robin Day's polypropylene chair, designed for Hille in 1963.

In 1956, plastics were used for the first time in the body of a car (the Citroën DS in 1956) and were also employed in the design of components for spacecraft.

12 Massey, op.cit., p. 155.

Above

Vitra Home Collection, 2004, by Studio Bouroullec. Although they are often transient elements, items of furniture can inform or define the material landscape of an interior. This arrangement, curated for furniture manufacturers Vitra by Studio Bouroullec, includes furniture designed by Ray and Charles Eames, Verner Panton, Gio Ponti, Arne Jacobson, Maarten Van Severen, and Jasper Morrison.

These advances were inspiring to many designers, who based their styling and selection of materials on these industries. This is illustrated in Alison and Peter Smithson's House of the Future:

Arguably the purest expression of the Smithsons' Pop ideology was the House of the Future, the visionary "model home" they devised for the 1956 Daily Mail Ideal Home Exhibition. Designed, predominantly by Alison, to be a plastic structure which could be mass-produced in its entirety, rather than in parts, the house included then-innovative futuristic features, such as a self-cleaning bath, easy-to-clean corners, and remote controls for the television and lighting.[13]

The moon landing of 1969 had a significant impact on public mood and the collective imagination. Popular culture embraced visions of the future and communicated them to the masses; the Space Age aesthetic was evident in music, fashion, and film, and was reflected in the materials of interior design.

The 1960s and 1970s saw an explosion in the production of highly developed plastics; artists and designers tested the potential of these materials, which were used in furniture, products, clothing, and domestic fabrics. Plastics were readily available and easily replaced ("disposable"), which corresponded with the Pop aesthetic and consumers' desire for the new—a pernicious condition that continues to pervade many societies.

Advances in technological and manufacturing processes (motivated by economic, scientific, and environmental imperatives) continue to transform the range of materials available for interior design today.

13 Design Museum website: http://designmuseum.org/design/alison-peter-smithson_(accessed 04.07.11).

Right
Thonet's Chair No. 14, one of the first mass-produced chairs, made of bent wood, has been in production since 1859.

3. The historical influence of the environmental agenda and its impact on materials

Contemporary designers' choice of materials is now informed by concerns about global warming and the depletion of natural resources—these themes are explored in Part 2 of this book. However, it is worth noting here that these concerns are not new and that the "green" agenda has had an influence on design for several decades.

Rachel Carson (1907–1964) was an American marine biologist, conservationist, and early environmentalist. Her book, *Silent Spring*, was first published in 1962. It recounts the destructive nature of human progression and describes a concern for human and animal welfare and the environment. Carson appeared before Congress in the United States in 1963, and appealed for new policies to protect the natural world.

The Green Movement and the emergence of the hippies influenced approaches to design. In the 1960s, Worldshops, Third World Shops, and Fair Trade stores were opened selling goods for interiors; between 1968 and 1972, the *Whole Earth Catalogue* was published in the United States, advertising goods for an environmentally aware counterculture. During this period, "ethnic" fabrics, carpets, and artifacts from non-Western cultures were used to furnish homes—these became statements of political identity and symbols of anti-Western capitalism (although still a form of consumerism).

Twenty years after the publication of Carson's book, Austrian-born designer and educator Victor Papanek published *Design for the Real World*. In the book he explores concerns about ecology but also writes about the social responsibility of designers.

These early proponents of the environmental movement gave impetus to the environmental agenda, pressurizing governments and industry. Their convictions led to the first shifts in government policy and also to changes in the materials used by manufacturers of products for interiors.

Concerns about the environment have also lead to an increasing tendency to reuse existing buildings as a way of conserving materials, a process that is described in Part 2 of this book. However, this approach has historical precedents, which are particularly relevant to contemporary designers working within existing buildings.

Italian architect and designer Carlo Scarpa is well known for his architectural interventions within historic buildings, including designs for the Castelvecchio Museum, Verona (1957–75) and the Querini-Stampalia Foundation, Venice (1961–3); these sites are critical references for the interior design student.

Scarpa's sensitive designs respond to the historical and physical context of the building, complementing and enhancing the qualities of the original space and expressing clear distinctions between existing and new materials. These spatial concepts are echoed in the articulation of the details and careful juxtapositions of materials.

Left and far left
At the Castelvecchio Museum, Verona, Carlo Scarpa made sensitive material interventions within an existing, historic building. Existing materials with their marks, scars, and "memories," are offset by new materials. Although there is a distinct separation of the old and the new, there is also a form of embrace as one material is wrapped around or enfolded by another.

4. The twenty-first century

In our Postmodern world, there is no single dominant style or design movement. Instead, each designer or design group adopts a very different approach to their use of materials, and there is an acceptance of pluralism and diversity. Designs draw upon an inclusive and eclectic array of multicultural sources and motivating influences. However, themes are emerging that may well unify this generation of designers, philosophically and conceptually if not stylistically: the environmental agenda, the global economic crisis, and the emerging political, social, and economic influences of countries and regions such as China, India, and South America. All could have an influence on the materials used in interior design.

In addition to these themes, digital technologies are revolutionizing how spaces are conceived, designed, refined, communicated, and constructed:

Much of the material world today, from the simplest consumer products to the most sophisticated airplanes, is created and produced using a process in which design, analysis, representation, fabrication, and assembly are becoming a relatively seamless collaboration process that is solely dependent on digital technologies—a digital continuum from design to production.[14]

This "digital continuum" has transformed the potential of materials. There has been a shift away from the Platonic solids and Euclidian geometries used in traditional architectural design and there is now an emergence of complex, curvilinear, and biomorphic forms.

Computer programs can also be used to test the performance of materials, for example, the acoustic properties of a material and the aural experience they create within an imagined interior, or the quality of light and its effect on the surface of materials.

The beginning of the twenty-first century has also seen the evolution and production of many new materials: plastics are becoming more environmentally friendly as biodegradable and compostable polymers have been invented; plastic and metallic materials that have "memory" are used in product design; and lightweight, translucent concretes have been developed. These themes and the emergence of new materials and processes are discussed in Part 5 of this book.

Part 1 has introduced some of the significant historical influences on the material qualities of interiors. The examples discussed in this section are by no means comprehensive; they are limited primarily to nineteenth- and twentieth-century design and they have a Western bias. However, they do suggest how interior design has evolved over the last 150 years and they offer a glimpse of the heritage of the contemporary practitioner.

14 Branko Kolarevic, ed., *Architecture in the Digital Age: Design and Manufacturing*, London and New York: Taylor & Francis, 2003, p. 7.

Below left
A visualization of an imagined interior by Zaha Hadid Architects.

Below center
For the London offices of Claydon Heeley Jones Mason, 2001, Ushida Findlay Architects designed complex ribbon-like forms from painted, rolled-steel ribbons. The ribbon served to unify disparate spaces within the office.

Below
The continuing advancements in materials science and methods of production have produced a new generation of innovative materials. Litracon, shown here, is a lightweight, translucent concrete.

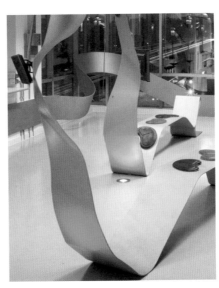

PART II SELECTION

We live in a world of materials; it is materials that give substance to everything we see and touch[1]

Design is an act of will, a considered response to an identified need or desire, a process that often results in a product, place, or space—a material solution. Ashby and Johnson state: "materials are the stuff of design,"[2] and it is this "stuff" that the interior designer must learn to test, understand, and manipulate before he or she is able to select materials for a particular context.

It is the process of material selection at the conceptual stages of a project that will be the focus of this part of the book—particularly how material selection relates to the project brief and client, the project site, and the exploration and development of design solutions.

1 Mike Ashby and Kara Johnson, *Materials and Design: The art and science of material selection in product design*, Oxford: Butterworth-Heinemann, 2002, p. 3.
2 Ibid., p. 55.

Below
Discussions about materials at the early stages of a project can inform the client's brief and set clear parameters for the designer.

5. The brief and client

Most interior design projects begin with a project brief—a description of a spatial need that has been identified by a client and/or a user group. The brief is often a "live" document that is analyzed and refined through an iterative process of design, discussion, and debate. On smaller projects, this process could be a simple dialog between the client and the interior designer; on larger projects, the process is likely to include input from other specialist consultants such as structural engineers; mechanical, electrical, and environmental engineers; lighting designers; graphic designers; cost consultants; and project managers.

The refined project brief is unlikely to make specific reference to materials but it will set parameters that will inform the selection of materials, which could include image or brand identity; cost, quality, or program; the emotions to be elicited; or functional, sensory, technical, or sustainable requirements.

Visual identity

The client may appoint a designer because they believe that designer's image and identity, defined through their portfolio and studio culture, to be sympathetic to their own: the designer may have a recognized style or use a vocabulary of materials that fit with the client's values and aspirations.

Alternatively, the designer might be appointed because they have demonstrated their ability to read, interpret, and expand the client's vision. This often happens when designers are invited to "pitch" for a project, usually a presentation to the client in which they make proposals in response to a brief in a bid to win a project. During this process designers will demonstrate their ability to translate the client's image or brand into an inspiring, innovative spatial design. This is a chameleon-like existence that can give the designer opportunities to work with a broad range of clients and on very different building types with contrasting material needs.

In each case, the designer may well respond to the brief by assembling a selection of reference images, colors, and materials that are an expression of the client's identity; the materials and images selected might correspond with client values such as "strength," "openness," or the need to appear "green." This selection of information might include key materials for the built environment, but could also incorporate materials and concepts associated with products, furniture, and graphic design: uniforms, logos, fonts, and packaging. This collection will be manipulated and honed until a palette has been agreed.

Not all clients will have a clearly defined image or identity, and it will be the designer's job to help the client define their vision. This is part of the development of the brief for the client. In this context, the designer has the freedom to propose alternative visual identities for the client and the venue or site. They can be playful with materials and propose innovative solutions. Materials and colors will be selected to create a particular atmosphere, or a one-off spatial experience that represents the "values" of the client.

Designers are often required to consider how a brand identity can be reinforced through the selection of color and materials. The following exercise can help the designer think laterally about material choices and how they can be used to create a particular image or to reinforce an existing brand.

Identify a client or brand for this exercise—perhaps a familiar chain retailer. Answer the following questions assuming that "I" represents the brand:

If I were a car I would be...
If I were a dog I would be...
If I were a item of clothing I would be...
If I were a plant I would be...
If I were a piece of furniture I would be...

- Reconsider your response to the questions, trying to avoid obvious answers or clichés. Does this change your answers in any way?

- Consider your answers and identify any shared characteristics or values that could be identified —perhaps create a list of words. How could these values translate into materials and colors? Do the words suggest particular material qualities? Types of supplier? An approach to details?

- Collect materials that correspond with the values and characteristics you have identified. How might the materials be used in the interior? What do they signify about the brand you have chosen?

It can be challenging to identify appropriate materials for different contexts and functions. A good way to extend your knowledge and to increase your confidence when selecting materials is to analyze existing uses of materials:

- Select and visit two existing buildings (preferably of some design merit) that have contrasting functions. For example, a hospital and a high-end retail outlet.

- Try to identify the materials used in each of the buildings for the same function: walls, floors, handrails, ceilings, etc.

- Compare the aesthetic, functional, and technical properties of the materials. What are the similarities and differences?

- Identify any apparent problems with the materials that have been specified. Are there any obvious cleaning or maintenance issues? How would you improve the specification of materials?

- Reflect upon your research and identify any significant findings that will inform your own choices about materials.

The table below lists the kinds of notes that you might take when following such an exercise.

Cost, quality, and program

The project brief will make reference to the client's vision for the interior but will also include other considerations, such as the budget (there is usually a "cost plan") and the program—important constraints for the designer.

On most projects there is usually a compromise between how much materials cost, the quality of the construction (how materials are assembled), and the speed at which the project is built. If speed is the priority, then the quality may need to be compromised and the project will cost less; if quality is the priority then the interior is likely to take longer to build and cost more.

The designer will need to understand the client's priorities before selecting materials. For example, if the client's brief describes a rapid program for a series of "roll-out" projects then the designer will need to check the availability of the materials selected to ensure that they can be delivered on time and within budget. Sometimes this process will involve the building contractor, in order to ensure that the different packages (discrete areas of work) are subcontracted in sufficient time to allow subcontractors to purchase and assemble materials. Additionally, if the project is intended as a temporary solution then this will affect the choice of materials, as a short-term solution could be less durable and so more cost-effective.

While the brief may not make specific reference to materials, designers will often have an intuitive understanding of appropriate material selections and combinations for the project. The palette selected needs to balance the functional, technical, aesthetic, and sensory properties of the materials—this is one of the great challenges for the interior designer and will be expanded on in the next section of the book.

Project	City hospital	High-end retail	Reflective notes
Walls	Painted plasterboard with protective rail at the height of trolleys. Issues: signs of wear and tear	Polished plaster, mirror, and digital media walls. Issues: cost	The materials used in the store are opulent and expensive—they reinforce the "quality" brand. The hospital is designed for durability, but paint and graphics are used to lift the atmosphere and to aid navigation.
Floors	Non-slip vinyl and ceramics. Issues: signs of wear and tear	Stone and cut-pile carpet. Issues: cost and source of stone	In both cases, the materials need to be durable and easy to clean; however, the store's materials are more expensive/opulent.
Ceilings	Perforated metal and timber slatted ceiling in public areas. Issues: cleaning	Painted perforated plasterboard. Issues: none	In both cases, acoustics have been considered; timber is used to add warmth to the public areas of the hospital; the store's ceilings are simple and cheap (the focus is on floors and walls).
Hardware	Acrylic. Issues: not durable enough	Satin-finished stainless steel. Issues: optical issues for partially sighted	The cheaper product used in the hospital is not of sufficient quality and will need to be replaced, possibly with a better-quality acrylic product or an alternative material.

6. The site

The project site may have been selected by the client before the interior designer is appointed, although this is not always the case. Sometimes the designer acts as the client's advisor when evaluating and choosing a site, and helps the client to negotiate the terms of a lease or purchase. It is also possible that the designer will be asked to make proposals for a generic site. This is often the case in retail design, and is referred to as a "roll-out" project. In this situation, a design will be adaptable to suit a range of different locations and will comprise a set of key details and a specification or list of material finishes.

However, for most projects the site is a central "character" and will have a direct influence upon the designer's concepts and choice of materials. Project sites vary greatly. They can be existing structures, newly constructed buildings, a proposed building that exists only in the form of models and drawings, a building under construction, or a temporary site. Every site has specific contextual issues that need to be carefully considered: there may be historical elements of a building that need to be retained or complemented through a design approach or proposal. Each will suggest a different material response.

Below
In their design for a studio in Rotterdam, Studio Rolf.fr in partnership with Zecc Architecten have made a clear distinction between the materials of the existing building and those of the new intervention. Existing brick walls were left untreated. New materials include painted timber floorboards, ⅛ in "blue plate" steel flooring with a waxed finish, a new painted timber stair, painted plaster walls, and coated aluminum sink units. Note the traditional chair wrapped in a polymeric material in the center image.

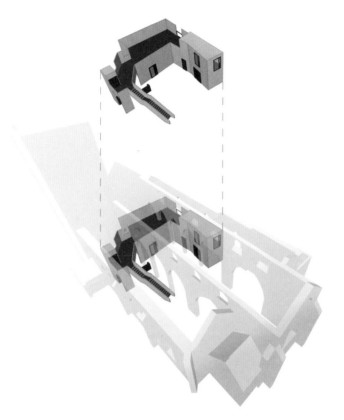

Existing buildings

An existing building will vary according to age, condition, architectural merit, and previous use, uses, or misuses. It could be a building that is well loved by the community, a "personality" that generations of the same family remember, a landmark in a city, a listed building, an anonymous structure lost in the complexities of the built environment or a hidden "jewel" waiting to be revived.

Each existing building will have its own material identity, which the designer inherits. The materials may be a source of inspiration to the designer, who may wish to reveal the essential character of the existing palette while juxtaposing it with the new. Alternatively, the designer may wish to conceal the existing materials under a veneer of the new.

In order to decide upon a strategy for the materials of the intervention, first the designer must analyze and understand the existing. In his book, *On Altering Architecture*, Fred Scott refers to this process as "stripping back":

Left and above left
For this museum project, Dow Jones Architects have made a sensitive insertion into an existing, historic building; the new materials provide a marked contrast with the existing stone and are designed to minimize damage to the host building. The insertion was constructed from Eurban prefabricated engineered panels of uncoated laminated solid timber; natural linoleum was used for the new floor at first-floor level. The axonometric diagram illustrates how the timber insertion fits into the host building.

Stripping back in its extended manifestation is the process by which the interventional designer acquires an understanding of the host building with which he or she is engaged. It is to the end of developing a structured affinity, as a preparation for the correspondence between their work and the existing. The host building needs to be understood intrinsically and in terms of its setting, and to be looked at in terms of actualities and provenance. This is an enquiry that will have both architectural and socio-economic aspects. It is proposed here as the foundation for all consecutive procedures.[3]

Scott goes on to define four areas of focus for the process of "stripping back": Materials, which is concerned with all material properties, including the structure and construction of the building; Spatial, which relates to spatial configurations, hierarchies, sequences, proportion, etc.; Style, which relates to the style of the building (i.e. Georgian) and historical exemplars; and finally the marks of previous occupants or "Palimpsest": the layered

marks and traces of subsequent users of the space and the memories the worn materials evoke or embody.

Understanding "of what and how the host building is made" enables the informed designer to define a clear concept or strategy for the materials of the intervention. Harmonious, antagonistic, unified, contrasting, separate, juxtaposed, seamless, intrusive, ephemeral, symbiotic, and parasitic are just a few of the approaches that have been attributed to strategies for inserting materials within an existing building.

In their project for LBi, in London's Truman Brewery, the designers, Brinkworth, exposed the essential material character of the existing building by revealing the muscular, gray, steel structure and dull red-brick walls; these materials were juxtaposed with those of the new insertion, which were refined materials with glossy, polished surfaces and saturated colors.

3 Fred Scott, *On Altering Architecture*, London: Routledge, 2008, p. 108.

Right
Design firm Brinkworth converted an old London brewery into offices for digital marketing agency LBi. These photographs describe the physical process of "stripping back" the space to reveal the essential materials and structure of the existing building; the materials of the new insertion act as a counterpoint to the industrial quality of the original site.

STEP BY STEP RECORDING MATERIALS IN AN EXISTING BUILDING

Interior designers often make an intervention within an existing building. In this context, it is important for the designer to undertake a thorough investigation of the existing site and record the materials of the host building using drawing and photography. The designer can then develop concepts and make informed decisions about the materials to be used for the intervention.

In this example, the Aspex Gallery, Portsmouth, UK, by Glen Howells Architects, is explored in order to gain a better understanding of its material qualities.

1 Begin by identifying what you need to understand about the site and its material qualities. For example, you might decide to record original materials; materials associated with any interventions, or extensions made to the original building; any damage or "scars" that have been left on materials, or signs of usage; the sensory nature of materials, including those used for structural purposes. Begin by making a photographic record.

2 In addition to photographs, make sketches of the space and begin to record the material quality (color, texture, light, and material relationships). Add your analytical notes.

3 Begin to focus on a particular material (in this case, brick). Complete more detailed drawings and close-up photographs. Record your analytical notes—these might include your notes about the condition of the material, its relationship with other materials within the space (joints and junctions) and its relationship to the external finishes.

4 You could also use some of your recordings as the basis for presentations at a later stage of the project: for example, sketching over photographs to generate perspective views of the space —these could be colored up in Photoshop, inserting human figures to show scale.

STEP BY STEP MAKING A SENSORY READING OF A SITE

This exercise can be completed at the beginning of a design project when analyzing an existing site. You should begin by identifying the senses you wish to represent (refer to pages 68–80 for suggestions). Aim to use a wide range of media, drawing types, diagrams, and notes to represent your sensory experience of the space. Consider how you can use line, point, color, pattern, shape, texture, tone, and form to communicate your experience. In this example a church was explored to gain a better understanding of its material qualities.

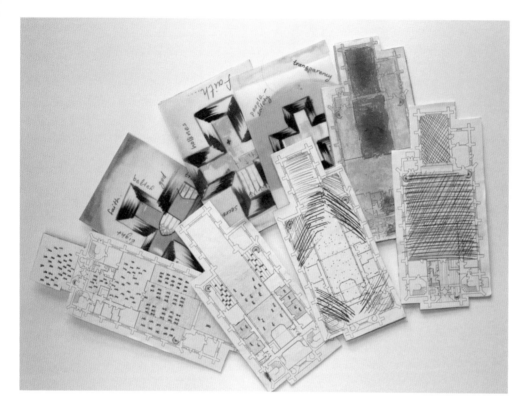

1 Use a set of small plans (thumbnail size) to record your initial observations. These diagrams could represent your reading of temperature, movement of people, light, and sound, etc.

2 Use a range of different media and techniques to represent your observations of color, light, tone, and pattern.

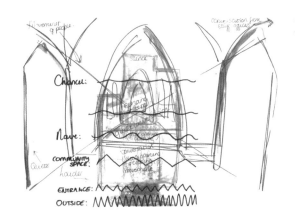

3 Experiment with alternative methods of representing sound and movement. When focusing upon a particular sense, take time to absorb your body's experience; for example, what can you hear? Listen to the sounds closest to you, those that are slightly removed, and those in the distance. How can you represent these shifts and layers of sound?

4 Experiment with color and collage in order to represent different textures and temperatures.

5 Make a painting or sculptural object that represents your personal response to the site: a conceptual portrait or "spirit of place" object.

6 Combine your drawings, notes, paintings, and collages in a "book," folder, or portfolio.

New buildings, proposed buildings, buildings under construction

If the project is a new building, either proposed or under construction, it is likely that the interior designer will be working as part of a multidisciplinary team, or one of several such design teams.

For example, when a new large shopping mall is being designed it will have a base-building design team for the overall structure, a fit-out design team for the public areas, and also design teams for the individual retail units. In this case, the different parties have to share information about materials; codes or guidelines for the use of materials in the public areas are often published, and there may well be constraints on how materials are used and assembled within the retail units.

When working on a new building, the interior designer may be introduced to the site when the base building has been completed or they may have worked on the design as part of a multidisciplinary team from the outset of the project. In the case of the former, the designer will inherit and respond to the materials palette of the new building; in the case of the latter, they will collaborate with other members of the team and negotiate the palette of materials to be specified (internally and externally) so that a robust and coherent proposal can be presented to the client.

Left and below left
BDP's West Lothian Civic Centre, Scotland, was designed by an integrated team of architects, interior designers, landscape architects, and acousticians. The civic space has an internal gable wall of Jura limestone and flooring of honed Burlington Brandy Crag slate. Wood, glass, and rich hues of burnt orange and lime green punctuate the interior.

Temporary sites

A temporary site is usually the scene of a one-off temporary design or intervention; however, this is not necessarily always the case. The design could be transient, moving from one temporary location to another. For example, an exhibition display unit may be used several times at different events and in different locations around the world, or a concept for a "pop-up" store could result in the same "interior" being used in several temporary sites, perhaps derelict buildings or empty retail units. The intervention may be fleeting and the material relationships between the "interior" and the temporary, host site are likely to be incidental—perhaps resulting in a collision of material identities or very separate, parallel entities, one paying little regard to and having little impact on the other.

Context

In addition to the character of the existing building, the designer must also consider the geographical location of a site. The physical context of the project (urban, suburban, or rural); the associated climate (hot, cold, arid, humid, etc.); the local architectural traditions; uses and sources of materials that might inform a vernacular approach to design; and the local community and their cultural and religious identities are all important factors that could influence the type of materials selected for the new intervention.

Along with issues such as budget and program, the brief and the site provide the creative constraints within which design concepts are developed.

Below
The overall budget for this temporary, pop-up store for Dr. Martens footwear was about $24,000. The designers, Campaign, used recycled and industrial materials and fluorescent lighting to display the merchandise.

7. The concept

The creative design process is a complex negotiation of issues involving the analysis and clarification of the project brief; an analysis and understanding of the site; and an attempt to reconcile the site and brief and progress with a solution—a process of synthesis. At this stage a feasibility study is often carried out to test and communicate the proposals. As a result of this, an evaluation and possible refinement of the solution may be necessary. This non-linear, iterative process, involving the client, the designer, and other consultants, may be repeated a number of times before a clear direction and design concept is agreed upon.

Play is an important part of this phase of a project, which ultimately has to marry creativity and logic, the aesthetic and the technical. During this playful period, the interior designer or design team will use a range of methods to generate and test ideas in their studio. For example, they might use mind-maps, diagrams, sketches, words, concept and spatial models, precedent images from magazines and books, images of the designer's own previous projects, and the design team might also surround themselves with "the stuff of design": color swatches, product catalogs, furniture catalogs and of course, samples of the materials themselves. These may be

Left and above
The way materials are stored can characterize a designer's studio and can encourage innovative practice.

familiar samples that reside in the studio, forming part of the studio's visual identity, or a collection of new materials that have been sourced specifically for the project from exhibitions or from manufacturers. Ashby and Johnson describe this process in the book, *Materials and Design*:

The picture that emerges is that of the designer's mind as a sort of melting pot. There is no systematic path to good design, rather, the designer seeks to capture and hold a sea of ideas and reactions to materials, shapes, textures, and colors, rearranging and combining these to find a solution that satisfies the design brief and a particular vision for fulfilling it.[4]

It can be very revealing to visit a designer's studio and observe this creative process in action. Some designers work in very formal, tidy, controlled environments but very often their working environment is more aligned with that of the art studio: walls are covered with reference images, notes, and drawings; inspirational objects and artifacts are collected and material samples pepper the space—propped against walls, under desks, and spread out on meeting tables—giving the studio its visual identity and design culture. This informality allows materials to be juxtaposed in unexpected ways, permits the conventions

of materials to be challenged, and encourages designers to play with alternatives.

In a fine-art context, materials and meaning are a vital component in communicating the concept behind a work; for example, Joseph Beuys (German, 1921–1986) juxtaposed symbolically "loaded" materials, such as felt and lard; Cildo Meireles (Brazilian, born 1948) uses materials and components including bones, money, and communion wafers to construct his installations; James Turrell (American, born 1943) uses light to create architectural space. A more extreme example is the British artist Marc Quinn (born 1964), who uses his own blood.

These theoretical and practical approaches to materials can be adopted by the interior designer to enrich and substantiate their conceptual thinking. Materials can be selected because they are imbued with meaning and values, because they can reinforce a narrative and symbolize an idea; materials communicate, and an audience responds consciously or subconsciously.

Other areas of design can also inform and influence material choice, including clothing and fashion design, which can be another inspiring starting point when developing material concepts for an interior.

4 Ashby and Johnson, op. cit., p. 50.

Left

The German-born American artist Eva Hesse (1936–1970) had a process-led approach to making art. She explored ordinary materials and found objects, as well as cutting-edge materials (at the time) such as resin and fiberglass. As Hesse's work exemplifies, by physically manipulating and working with materials their possibilities and potential become apparent. By using materials that already exist the artist/designer can draw on the meaning associated with the material's previous state and invest the new form with a translation or interpretation of this meaning.

The Austro-Hungarian architect Adolf Loos (1870–1933) was pioneering in his focus on the relationship between fashion and architecture, both of which he saw as having evolved from early man's development of textile coverings for their bodies and more complex textile structures for shelter. Both disciplines came from a need for protection.

Hussein Chalayan (born 1970) is a British/Turkish-Cypriot fashion designer and is recognized for his innovative approach to materials, pattern cutting, and use of new technologies to generate form. He has spoken of his interest in both science and technology and architecture. Many of his designs have both symbolic and spatial, architectural qualities, making reference to human dislocation, furniture, and product design. The detail of his garments, fixings, and fastenings plays with the relationship between clothing and the interior: a skirt becomes a table, dresses have doors and decorations combine with structure.

Fashion design borrows from the language of spatial design but the interior designer can also borrow from the language of fashion, consider: the sensory qualities of cloth (innovative architextiles—digitally conceived and produced—are informing contemporary interiors)[5]; fixings and fastenings such as zippers, buttons, hooks, and eyes; the process and associated vocabulary of pattern cutting and assembly in order to create form; wrapping, folding, pleating, stitching, and weaving fabric. All of these processes and techniques may be applied to the materials of an interior and can be generators for spatial concepts.

5 Mark Garcia, ed., *Architextiles*, London: John Wiley & Sons, Publisher, 2006.

Left and far left
Some of Hussein Chalayan's fashion collections make reference to the materials and forms of spatial and product design. This garment contracts to form a "coffee table" and makes reference to transient and displaced people who need to carry their belongings with them.

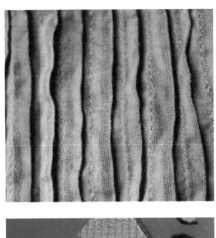  

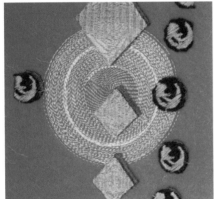  

This page

The language of fashion and textiles can provide inspiration when selecting and detailing materials for an interior: for example, the way fabrics are cut and assembled to create form and enclosure; fixings and fastenings such as buttons and zippers; threads, pleats, and laces.

As well as drawing inspiration by looking at the work of other practitioners, designers might collaborate with others to produce innovative material solutions. Tactility Factory is a company that represents the professional collaboration of Trish Belford (a textile designer) and Ruth Morrow (an architect). They apply interdisciplinary or crossover approaches to create unusual and inventive products for interiors. Girli Concrete, one of their products, challenges the perception of textiles as the "dressing" to structure and instead integrates textile technologies into the production of building products (concrete) to create innovative "soft" building surfaces. Its conceptual aim is to introduce "mainstream tactility" in the built environment. A similar, experimental approach is taken by Hazel Hewitt and her experiments with "knitted" concrete.

Right, top row
Trish Belford and Ruth Morrow combine their knowledge of textiles and architecture to create a new tactile product for interiors.

Right, bottom two rows
Hazel Hewitt tests the aesthetic potential of concrete, creating a "knitted" product with integrated fiberoptic lighting; her aim is to shift our perceptions of concrete, a material that can often be viewed negatively.

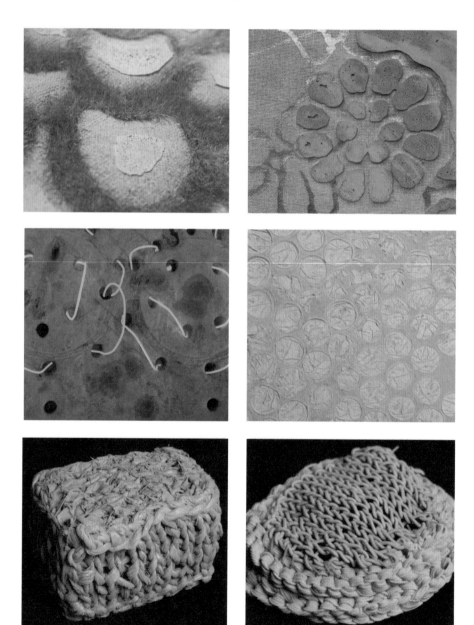

Designers develop spatial concepts in response to the client's values, image, and identity, the project brief, and the project site. It is often assumed that spatial concepts are defined as forms and then the appropriate surface or material is selected for its particular properties—that materials follow form. This is certainly one approach, but it need not be the case. The concept and the materials palette could be developed concurrently, or the material could be the generator for a spatial solution. The designer might identify a new, innovative material, which has not been used before, that suggests new spatial concepts, or might use a familiar material that has been appropriated from another context; form and spatial concepts could follow experiments with materials.

The next part of the book will introduce more factors that designers consider as they select and apply materials.

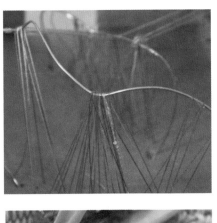

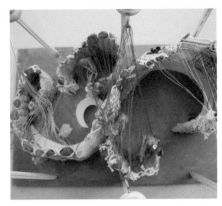

This page

In this project a student began by experimenting with materials and exploring the potential of thread: knitting, weaving, and stitching. Her experiments resulted in a spatial proposition: a woven enclosure made from recycled clothing (bottom right image).

STEP BY STEP SURFACE TO FORM

Concepts for interior space can be developed in response to a project brief and/or the project site. However, a spatial concept could also develop from experiments with materials and the forms they can create. This exercise begins with playful and analytical experiments with paper; the process allows for accidental or unpredictable discoveries that can fuel the imagination.

 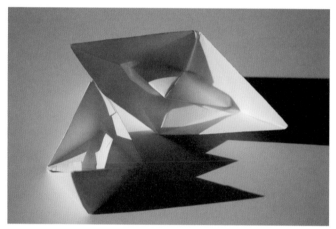

1 List as many different methods as you can that could be used to transform a piece of paper from a flat surface to a three-dimensional form. Start to experiment with sheets of paper by testing and analyzing contrasting methods of manipulating the surface: fold, cut, rip, score, puncture, weave, wrap, etc.

2 Record your experiments using sketching, light, and photography. Use these photographs to analyze the forms and spaces you have created. Compare qualities of solid and void, light and dark, open and closed, etc. Can you imagine an interior application for the form?

3 Remake the form or space by using a variety of different materials. In this image, acetate and wire have been used. Do these contrasting materials alter your reading of the space or form? Imagine it at the scale of a product, the scale of a room, and the scale of a city. What could it be?

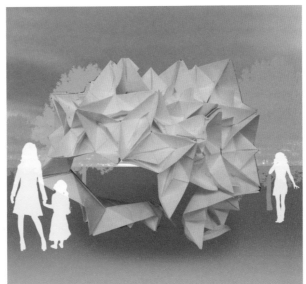

4 Using hand drawing, collage, photography, or photomontage, describe alternative applications for your form or space.

STEP BY STEP COMBINING MATERIALS

Creative uses of materials can emerge from a playful
approach in the early stages of a project. This exercise
encourages an exploration of material differences,
and of how juxtapositions of contrasting materials
can suggest exciting possibilities for interiors.

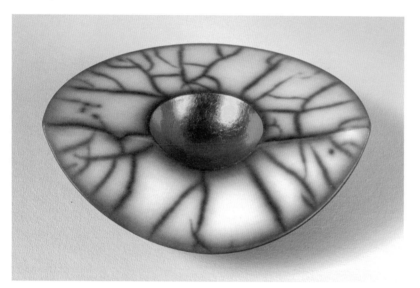

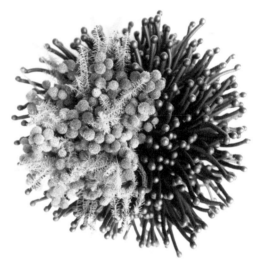

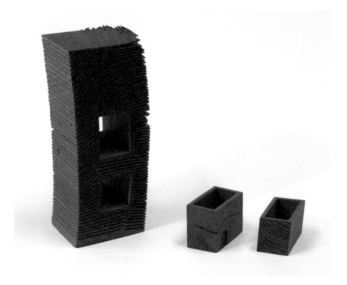

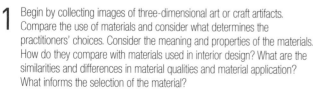

1 Begin by collecting images of three-dimensional art or craft artifacts.
Compare the use of materials and consider what determines the
practitioners' choices. Consider the meaning and properties of the materials.
How do they compare with materials used in interior design? What are the
similarities and differences in material qualities and material application?
What informs the selection of the material?

Sculptures by, clockwise from top left: Emma Johnstone, Junko Mori
(*No. 60 Organism*, 2002), Will Spankie (*Clam*, carved alabaster), and David
Leefe Kendon (*Double Drawer*, cut from oak, 2007).

 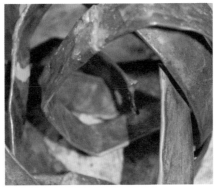 

2 Having considered the various qualities and potential meanings of materials, collect samples and pair materials that have contrasting qualities (strong and fragile, opaque and transparent, rough and smooth, etc.). The objects shown here combine plastic and metal, stone and metal, and stone and wood.

3 Using the pairs of materials, experiment with alternative methods of combining, joining, and fixing the materials (avoid using glue). Record your processes using sketching and photography. These projects incorporate woven wire and glass fragments, and woven cotton and plastic thread.

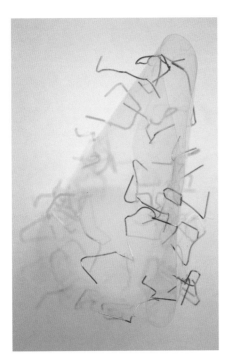  

4 Choose your preferred pair of materials and create a three-dimensional composition that expresses the material differences. Consider how these experiments might inform your approach to using materials in an interior. Do they suggest possibilities for creating or detailing spatial interventions?

In these examples metal is combined with paper, clay, and wood.

PART III APPLICATION

Below left and bottom

Theatrical events such as a fashion show can provide opportunities for designers to create innovative, temporary structures. In this set for a fashion launch by Gloss Creative Pty Ltd and LAVA (Laboratory for Visionary Architecture) the designers generated an 59 ft x 16 ft shell from 2,000 pieces of precisely cut pine.

Below right

In another set for the same fashion retailer (by Gloss Creative with producers Rizer and graphic designers Qualia Creative & Kimberley Witkowski) looped and "knotted" acetate and quilling paper was used to create this sculptural form.

As the designer moves beyond the conceptual phase of a project, ideas begin to crystallize and detailed designs develop. At this stage, designers will begin to apply a rigorous analysis of the materials selected and evaluate material qualities and their suitability for various applications. This will include the consideration of a material's properties within the overall context of a project (both functional and aesthetic) and also material details: juxtapositions, joints and junctions, fixings and fastenings, assembly and construction.

8. Material properties

Property: a quality or characteristic attribute,
such as the density or strength of a material[1]

An experienced designer will often respond to a
material intuitively, and will have an understanding
of its suitability for various applications. However, it is
important for the designer to question these judgments
and to ensure they have a full understanding of a
material's properties when applied in different contexts;
for example, understanding whether the material is
durable or fragile, acoustically absorbent or resonant.
The designer must gain this knowledge in order to make
informed judgments about the material's suitability and its
relationship to the selected palette for a particular project
or scheme. Questioning your preconceptions
and challenging conventions can also lead to more
innovative practice.

There is also the possibility of using materials from
other areas of design. Materials from car manufacture and
production, packaging, and other commercial applications
can also be used in an interiors context. A designer needs
to look at materials creatively and critically analyze them
to consider new possibilities.

When assessing a material for a particular use, you
might consider the following properties: functional,
relative, sensory, environmental, and subjective. These
characteristics are expanded below.

Functional properties

When selecting materials, the designer must balance
aesthetic judgments with the technical and functional
requirements of a project. The functional requirements
will vary according to the context; for example, the
demands on materials used in a design for a temporary
exhibition, set, or pop-up store will be very different to
those used in a more permanent context.

The transient nature of some interior interventions
or designs can liberate the designer to take risks and
experiment with materials. Conventions can be challenged
and the limitations and possibilities of materials can be
tested. The designer may not be too concerned about the
durability of materials, but other functional and aesthetic
characteristics will take priority. A number of contemporary
practitioners have seized such opportunities to create
impermanent, innovative interiors, as illustrated by the
projects on the following pages.

When designing a more "permanent" interior—
for example, a hospital, school, or museum—material
specification can become an onerous responsibility.
Once designers complete such a project, they leave

1 *Collins English Dictionary and Thesaurus*, Twenty-first Century Edition,
London: Harper Collins, 2003.

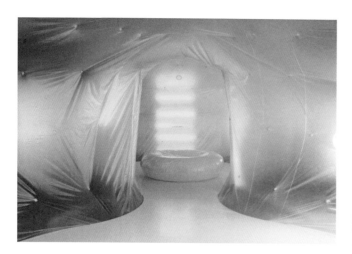

This page

Veech Media Architecture is a research-based design practice based in Vienna. Using innovative materials and new methods of construction, these architects design transient structures and forms for exhibitions and events across the globe. They combine contemporary materials technology with sophisticated media systems to create multisensory, immersive environments. Examples include the "Global Tools" exhibition installation, Helsinki, Finland, 2002 (shown above and above right) and the award-winning "Ambient Gem" exhibition installation, designed for Swarovski ENLIGHTENED™, Basel, Switzerland, 2008 (shown right). The pavilion is constructed using a translucent, pneumatic material, inflated in facets to create a crystalline form. The functional requirements of a material in this context are to provide a temporary, branded enclosure that can be easily transported and assembled. While the structure is not permanent (and resilience and maintenance of materials are not primary concerns), the designers will have considered the need to transport and assemble the materials (possibly more than once) as well as the need to withstand the touch of numerous curious visitors.

This page
The Ice Hotel in Sweden presents an extreme example of transient materials used for an interior. Each year the hotel is sculpted and formed from ice by artists and designers; it melts in the summer and is reformed by different artists and designers in the winter: an annual process of renewal that mirrors the seasons.

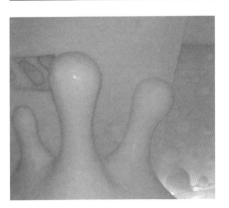

Below left
The materials selected for the
Royal Alexandra Children's Hospital
in Brighton, UK (designed by BDP)
were carefully chosen for their
aesthetic qualities, durability, and
ease of cleaning and maintenance.

Below right
A stone step in Istanbul, Turkey,
worn over time by abrasive
footsteps.

clients with a material legacy. The clients will "live"
with the materials; their experience may be enhanced by
the materials the designer has selected or they may be
frustrated by inadequate, inappropriate specifications that
need constant maintenance, repair, or, in the worst cases,
replacement. When tackling this context, designers can
still challenge material conventions but they must also
consider the longevity of materials and be confident that
the materials are durable, resilient, and maintainable with
reasonable effort and cost to the client: the materials must
be fit for purpose.

When designing for longevity, the interior designer
must also consider how a material will change over time as
a result of its function: a wooden balustrade will become
worn and molded by the touch of many hands, metal
door handles will develop a push–pull patina and stone
steps will erode under abrasive feet. The way the material
"wears" will give the space a lasting sense of identity.

Below left
The materials selected for the
Royal Alexandra Children's Hospital
in Brighton, UK (designed by BDP)
were carefully chosen for their
aesthetic qualities, durability, and
ease of cleaning and maintenance.

Below right
A stone step in Istanbul, Turkey,
worn over time by abrasive
footsteps.

It connects the space with the user, and the material responds to day-to-day use:

Wood has its own odor, it ages, it even has parasites, and so on. In short, it is a material that has being. Think of the notion of "solid oak"—a living idea for each of us, evoking as it does the succession of generations, massive furniture, and ancestral family homes.[2]

These material changes can enhance the character of an interior; they are equivalent to the scars and wrinkles that appear on the body, marks that record the passage of time, personal histories, and experience.

Materials will fulfill numerous functional requirements (see pages 141–55 on classification). However, it is important to note that some of the functional properties of materials are governed by codes and legislation. Legislative documents describe how materials will need to function in order to provide inclusive environments and to minimize the risk to health and safety of the users: for example, to reduce the surface spread of flame or to minimize the risk of falling. This applies to materials that can be seen but also to those materials beneath the surface: leveling compounds, substrates, infill, framing systems, etc.

It is the designer's job to specify all of these components and to ensure they perform adequately. This can be daunting but there is plenty of reference material and literature that can be researched and analyzed, and specialist suppliers who can offer advice. There are no global standard documents, so designers must become acquainted with the legislation in the country in which they are working.

2 Jean Baudrillard, quoted in Mark Taylor and Julieanna Preston, *INTIMUS: Interior Design Theory Reader*, London: John Wiley & Sons Ltd, 2006, p. 40.

TIP SPECIFIC FUNCTIONS

Durability and maintenance are primary considerations when assessing functional performance of materials. However, there are many more criteria associated with a material's function that are too numerous to list in full, but which might include:

Acoustic properties materials that absorb or reflect sound, or that can provide acoustic separation between different spaces

Strength in compression or tension materials that can be used to provide structure

Hygiene materials that are specifically designed to reduce the risk of infection or contamination: for example, in an industrial kitchen

Light transmitting or emitting materials that can be used to conduct light, and can have different degrees of translucency and opacity

Water resistance materials that resist the penetration of water

Safety materials that reduce the risk of injury, e.g. non-slip flooring in a swimming pool

Thermal properties materials that provide insulation in order to reduce the energy required to heat or cool a space

Fire resistance materials that resist the surface spread of flame or the progress of fire

Relative properties

Materials react with one another and have their own radiance, so that the material composition gives rise to something unique. Material is endless.[3]

One of the great pleasures and significant skills associated with interior design is the ability to compose materials in three dimensions. Good interior designers will be attuned to the sensory nature of materials and have an understanding of color theory and tone. They will understand the unique properties of the individual materials selected, but also how these relate to each other technically and aesthetically:

There's a critical proximity between materials, depending on the type of material and its weight. You can combine different materials in a building, and there's a certain point where you find they are too far away from each other to react, and there's a point too where they are too close together, and that kills them.[4]

The designer's challenge is to orchestrate a palette of materials, to form a cohesive whole that has rhythm, tone, balance, counterpoint, harmony, or discord. Materials convey meaning, evoke memories, and create atmosphere; the parallels with music and art are clear, and it is helpful to consider the vocabulary associated with these fields when assembling a material palette.

3 Peter Zumthor, *Atmospheres*, Basel: Birkhäuser, 2006, p. 25.
4 Ibid., p. 27.

Right
At Monsoon restaurant, Sapporo, Japan, designed by Zaha Hadid Architects, a "tornado" of red and yellow swirls up toward the ceiling. Black biomorphic sofas provide a counterpoint, creating a dissonant jazz-like symphony of form and color.

Left
Studio Bouroullec's *Textile Field* installation at the Victoria and Albert Museum, London, 2011. The installation, made from colored foam and textiles, applies the concept of rhythm and repeat pattern, providing a counterpoint to the host structure.

TIP SHARED VOCABULARY OF MUSIC AND ART

Chord the simultaneous sounding of a group of musical notes, usually three or more in number

Color the use of all the hues in painting as distinct from composition, form, and light and shade. The distinctive tone of a musical sound

Composition the harmonious arrangement of the parts of a work of art in relation to each other

Counterpoint the musical texture resulting from the simultaneous sounding of two or more melodies or parts

Discord the harsh, confused mingling of sounds

Rhythm a harmonious sequence or pattern of masses alternating with voids, of light alternating with shade, of alternating colors, etc.

Tone the effect of the color values and gradations of light and dark in a picture

Definitions from *Collins English Dictionary and Thesaurus*, Twenty-first Century Edition, Harper Collins, 2003

In his book, *On Altering Architecture*, Fred Scott refers to the relevance of fine-art practice to interior design and the resemblance between the use of collage and intervention within an existing building:

The similarities between collage and intervention make available to the designer a range of practices and strategies common to the artist, especially the use of the accidental and the improvisational in carrying through the work. Both are the processes of making a composition from disparate elements, old and new, found and given. The similarities between the interventional composition and the work of the Synthetic phase of Cubism must be apparent.[5]

The use of collage in art has also had a significant influence on interior design. The practice began in the early twentieth century with the work of Georges Braque (French, 1882–1963) and Pablo Picasso (Spanish, 1881–1973). Both overlaid "found" images and materials to create a newly constructed image. This technique of sticking or layering materials has been adopted by others such as the German artist Kurt Schwitters (1887–1948) and the British designer Ben Kelly.

In many of his projects Ben Kelly composes material palettes as though assembling a three-dimensional collage, resulting in juxtapositions of materials that balance color, tone, and texture. While not consciously referencing particular paintings or artworks, the influence of art practice and theory on his work is evident and the parallels are clear.

Paintings can be a source of inspiration when composing materials. The artist can teach the designer about the use of color and how color affects moods and emotions (see page 68 on sensory properties). Paintings can also suggest how to balance saturated and neutral colors, complementary or harmonious colors, and light and dark tones. An artist's appreciation of proportion needs to be applied to the selection of material patterns and contrasting textures such as hard and soft.

The designer must also consider how material scales relate to each other within a space. For example, an unrelieved expanse of one material may be offset by smaller components of a contrasting material. The designer must also be aware of how the scale of a modular material such as brick or mosaic tile will relate to the overall scale of the "room"—the reading or experience of brick will be very different depending on the size of a space.

5 Fred Scott, *On Altering Architecture*, Routledge, 2008, p. 156.

Left
In her painting, *Sony (Los Angeles)* 2004, Sarah Morris positions complementary and harmonious colors to create tension, rhythm, and counterpoint. A similar use of color can be seen in Ben Kelly's design for the Produktion offices (opposite).

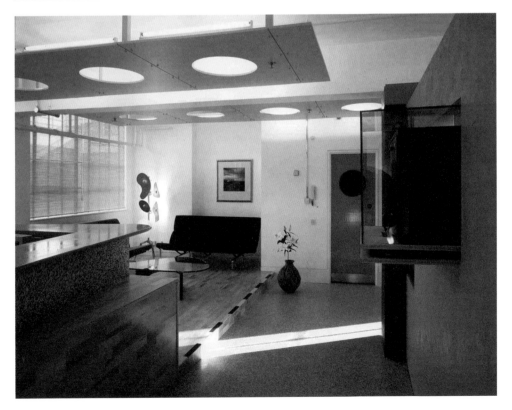

This page

In his designs for the Produktion Film Company, London (1995), Ben Kelly collages materials to create layers of texture and color. His methods reflect the practice of collage artists and suggest a painter's understanding of color.

As outlined in the first part of this book, an interior design project is likely to occur in one of three situations: a new building, realized or imagined; a transient location; or an existing building that has had one or more previous uses. In each situation, there is an existing material environment which the designer inherits and which will be in dialog with the material palette of the new interior intervention. As a consequence, the designer must decide how the materials of the intervention will relate to the inherited context. Material palette and forms may be in harmony or tension; the new intervention may appear symbiotic or parasitic; new materials may reveal or conceal the properties of the inherited; they may be sympathetic and complementary, or juxtaposed and aggressive in their contrast.

In addition to orchestrating the palette for "built-in" materials, the interior designer must also consider the material quality of surface treatments, "loose" furniture, objects, and artifacts, and determine how they relate to the whole. Items such as chairs, tables, rugs, light shades, and blinds furnish a room and welcome habitation.

While more fugitive elements, such as furniture (the "classic" chair being a good example) and products, may initially be designed or selected by the designer to cohere with and relate to the overall materials palette, over time they will be moved, altered, replaced, or augmented. This is the dynamic process of occupation, the animation of an interior:

The individual pieces exhibit varied treatments, materials, and finishes. … The various elements are intended to stand on their own, capable of being moved about at will without fundamentally altering the character of the room.[6]

The idea of things that have nothing to do with me as an architect taking their place in a building, their rightful place—it's a thought that gives me insight into the future of my buildings: a future that happens without me. That does me a lot of good. It's a great help to me to imagine the future of rooms in a house I'm building, to imagine them actually in use. In English you could probably call it "a sense of home."[7]

6 Taylor and Preston, op. cit., p. 188.
7 Zumthor, op. cit., p. 39.

Below and below right
The referencing of the traditional library can be seen in the contemporary interior by Elding Oscarson for the Stockholm-based magazine and web design bureau Oktavilla. Design journals are used as a material to create a partition, providing visual and acoustic separation as well as giving the studio a unique visual identity and referencing the client's business.

In this project for the D'Espresso Café in New York, which also references the traditional library, nemaworkshop reimagined the concept of the library by rotating it through 90 degrees: the traditional parquet flooring has become a wall, and photographs of books printed onto ceramic tiles line the wall and floor; finally, pendant lights project from the wall instead of hanging down vertically.

Other interior objects of a modest scale may be overlooked when composing a materials palette, but can have a significant impact on the material quality of an interior. These objects may be decorative, but could also be unpredictable, personal possessions that reveal the identity of the user or occupier.

In his essay, "A Wall of Books," William Braham notes:

Elsie de Wolfe [American, 1865–1950], too, understood books as a means of introducing colorful variety into the neutral/natural palette acceptable for the masculine stereotype of the library. "Here, if anywhere, you would think a monotony of brown wood would be obvious, but think of thousands of books with brilliant bindings. … Can't you see that this cypress room is simply glowing with color." [8]

8   Taylor and Preston, op. cit., p. 60.

Plants, both internal and external, and artwork can also add meaning, color, and texture—transient material qualities that alter as a result of organic changes or the process of augmentation, addition, and subtraction. Digital projection has also become an important and dynamic method of shaping interiors, as visual imagery, color, and light appear and disappear.

The materials palette, and how materials relate to each other, will elicit a physical, and possibly an emotional, response from users as they respond to the atmosphere created and the sensory nature of the materials selected.

Right and below right
Projection—used here for a music awards ceremony designed by LAVA (Laboratory for Visionary Architecture)—can transform an interior as materials, light, colors, and patterns become dynamic, acting as shifting influences on our experience of space.

Top
Waterlooville Children's Library, Hampshire, UK, designed by Hampshire County Architects in collaboration with artist Eileen White: artists are often commissioned to make an intervention within an interior using materials, color, pattern, and form to enhance the spatial experience.

Above
At the British Telecommunications headquarters in Watford, UK, BDP's interior design team worked with artist David MacIlwaine, who used light-edge acrylic, stainless-steel weights, and cables to create a kinetic intervention.

Above
Abbotts Ann Primary School, Hampshire, UK, by Hampshire County Architects: external planting can be used to "color" an interior as views of organic materials, texture, shape, and pattern soften the boundaries between inside and out; internal materials might also be designed and colored to reflect the natural world seen outside.

Sensory properties

Every touching experience of architecture is multi-sensory; qualities of space, matter, and scale are measured equally by the eye, ear, nose, skin, tongue, skeleton, and muscle. Architecture strengthens the existential experience, one's sense of being in the world, and this is essentially a strengthened experience of self. Instead of mere vision, or the five classical senses, architecture involves several realms of sensory experience which interact and fuse into each other.[9]

When selecting materials for an interior, the designer must consider the phenomenology of space: how the user will experience and respond to the sensory qualities of space, both physically and emotionally. This could include responses such as how it feels to touch a surface, or memories that are provoked, perhaps, by a smell or a particular sound. These experiences tend to be interconnected and holistic.

Traditionally, "the sensory" refers to the five classical senses (definitions attributed to Aristotle): sight, smell, touch, taste, and hearing. In addition to these familiar senses, many others have been identified including: sense of movement; balance; proprioception, or sense of self (our position in space); sense of life/comfort (well-being); and numinous, a sense of awe and wonder—these are all attributes to be cultivated by the designer.

In his book, *The Eyes of the Skin*, Juhani Pallasmaa argues that in Western society sight is privileged above the other senses, which have become suppressed—a phenomenon referred to as ocularcentrism. He claims this preferencing of sight in spatial design has led to an impoverished architectural landscape that does not permit full multi-sensory engagement with our environment—a form of sensory deprivation or under-stimulation.

There is now a shared recognition among practitioners from very different backgrounds (artists, designers, dancers, psychologists, etc.) that "the body" and its sensory readings or perceptions of space have been neglected and undervalued in the built environment. There is also an understanding that our senses do not exist and respond in isolation: science has proven that there is a complex crossover between the senses and that, for example, we "touch" with our eyes; "taste" with our nose; and "see" and "hear" with our skin.

Contemporary definitions of "the sensory" also recognize the subjective nature of spatial experience, and there is an understanding that our bodies carry with them memories: physiological, neurological, historical, sociological, and imagined. These memories color our readings and responses.

When assessing a material's properties for use in a particular project, the designer should consider the sensory qualities of that material and the atmosphere that will be created when materials are juxtaposed in three dimensions. Materials could be used to create holistic, multi-sensory experiences or to engage a particular sense or senses. We have used the five senses, below, to explore some of these possibilities.

Sight

When assessing the visual impact of a material the designer needs to understand the effects of light, which allows us to visually perceive depth, form, texture, color, shape, translucency, transparency, and opacity. The emissivity of a surface, its reflective qualities, and its impact on space are also important.

Light alters space in dramatic ways: it can change the color, "temperature," and atmosphere of a space; it can change our perceptions of volume, scale, and form; it can impact our emotions, well-being, and our ability to perform; and as light levels change throughout the day and seasonally there can be a corresponding shift in our energy levels and our mood.

The quality of light varies as we move across hemispheres, and between longitudes and latitudes; materials selected for a building in the northern hemisphere, where we experience dramatic seasonal contrasts, will have a very different character if used in latitudes where the seasons are constant. Light transforms materials and our reading of space, and it can also be used as a material itself, to create boundaries, destinations, rhythm, pace, and narrative; light can illuminate and shape the "stage" on which people perform their daily rituals, celebrate, play, grieve, contemplate, and commune.

9   Juhani Pallasmaa, *The Eyes of the Skin: Architecture and the Senses*, London: John Wiley & Sons Ltd, 2005, p. 41.

Left

Kunsthaus, Bregenz, Austria, by Peter Zumthor. The space is defined by the quality of light and shadow and the interaction between the contrasting surfaces of hard concrete and semi-translucent glass.

Left and far left

These images by students convey the dramatic and atmospheric potential of light and shade as light filters through windows, textiles, and decorative frames; light is a "material" that can be manipulated by the designer.

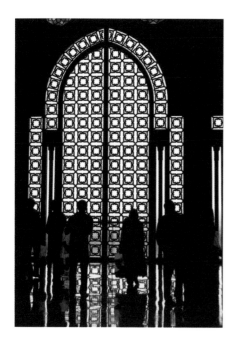

Above
Materials can be designed to
enhance the interplay between
light and form, creating dramatic
lighting effects that can define
an interior.

Below
Light and color are reflected in the
highly polished flooring material
at the Mandarina Duck Flagship
Store, Paris, 2001 by NL Architects
with Droog Design. This effect
can be achieved using polished
concrete, stone, or poured resin-
based materials.

Tonal composition in space is achieved through the
manipulation of natural light, artificial light, and also the
color and tone of the materials selected; slight adjustments
to any one of these ingredients can transform the spatial
experience. It may be the designer's intention to create
a dark, introspective, or contemplative environment
that envelops the occupant, or to create a light uplifting
environment that has fluid connections between inside
and out. In each case, very different materials and lighting
strategies will be adopted.

James Turrell is an installation artist who explores
the potential of natural and artificial light: "I'm interested
in playing with not only the physical limits of how we
perceive, but the learned limits." Light is the material
he uses to transform visual perceptions and experiences
of space.

In their design for Munich Re Group Headquarters,
artist Keith Sonnier, with architects Baumschlager and
Eberle, has used artificial lighting to dramatic effect.
Applying an understanding of color theory (in this case,
complementary color), and possibly drawing inspiration
from the fine-art practice of James Turrell, they have
designed an interior that is saturated with colored neon
light. Their use of a reflective flooring material enhances
the immersive qualities of this "painted" interior.

Artists Mark Rothko (American, 1903–1970),
Richard Diebenkorn (American, 1922–1993), Bridget
Riley (British, born 1931), Paul Klee (Swiss, 1879–1940),
and Patrick Heron (British, 1920–1999) serve as
particularly good examples of how the use of color in
painting can inspire a range of color compositions in an
interior. Their work, and that of many other painters, has
influenced interior designers. Paintings can be interpreted
to create atmospheric, cohesive, and complex interiors,
created through the careful juxtaposition of color, tone,
and lighting.

 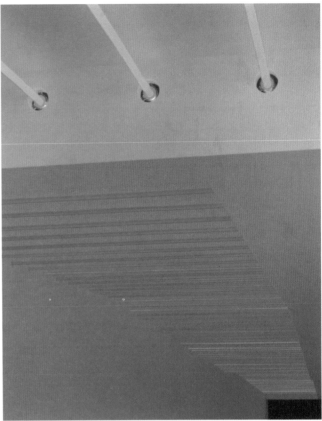

Above and above left
Munich Re Group Headquarters,
Munich. Artist Keith Sonnier,
with architects Baumschlager
and Eberle, has created a
permanent installation using neon
lighting. The light and color has
transformed a long passageway
that links two buildings, to create
an immersive, "painted" interior.

In their book, *Color: Communication in Architectural Space*, Meerwein, Rodeck, and Mahnke discuss the psychological effects of color and suggest that spaces can be visually understimulating or overstimulating:

Under- and overstimulation are opposite poles between which a certain perceived amount of information is experienced. The amount of visual stimuli (colors, patterns, contrasts etc.), extreme monotony and sensory deficiency can lead to understimulation, while an extreme surplus of stimuli can produce overstimulation. Overstimulation can trigger physical or psychological changes. On the physical level, breathing or pulse frequencies can be affected; blood pressure and muscle tension may increase. Studies have shown that people who suffer from understimulation displayed signs of restlessness, irritability, difficulties in concentrating, and perception disorders. ...

Berlyne and McDonnell discovered that diverse, inharmonious, and chaotic patterns led to an increase in the degree of stimulation.[10]

10 G. Meerwein, B. Rodeck, and F. Mahnke, *Color: Communication in Architectural Space*, Basel: Birkhäuser, English edition, 2007, pp. 22 and 23.

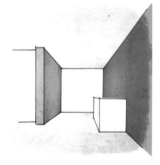 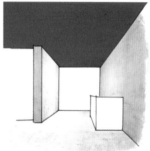 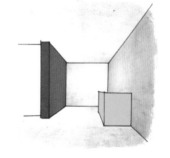 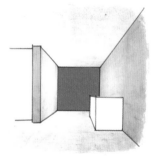

It is important for the designer to understand the
psychological impact that visual stimuli can have on
the occupant of a room or place. Colored and patterned
materials can be used to communicate cultural and
religious identities, wealth, and status; they can be
used to calm people and encourage them to relax, or
to stimulate and energize them. Consider the visual
differences between materials used in a restaurant,
which encourage customers to linger and immerse
themselves in the dining experience, and in cafés, which
encourage a rapid turnover. Such differences are likely
to include other senses too: acoustic, smell, touch, etc.

Attitudes toward the use of visually patterned and
decorative materials vary according to function, place,
time, and culture. In the West and more widely, there is
currently a resurgence of the decorative, wherein color and
pattern are being used to create "immersive" interiors. This
is perhaps a response to new technologies; fashion trends
that have revived the art and design of the 1950s, 60s,
and 70s; and also to counter the influence of Modernism.

The Modernist philosophy eschewed decoration, creating
minimalist interiors, an approach embraced by many in
the architectural and design community of the period but
perhaps not so enthusiastically by the wider community.

Above and left

The twenty-first century has witnessed a resurgence of the highly decorated, immersive interior; this can be seen in the wallpaper designs of Cole and Son ("Hick's Hexagon" is illustrated on the left) and in the work of Marcel Wanders at Villa Moda in Bahrain (above). Wanders distorts and enlarges traditional patterns, and the scale of familiar materials and forms are exaggerated in his designs.

STEP BY STEP UNDERSTANDING COLOR

Color is an integral quality of any material, and it is important that the designer understands color theory and is able to use color to define three-dimensional space. This sequence suggests methods of developing knowledge of color theory and testing alternative approaches to using color in space. If you have no recent knowledge of color theory, research and understand the basics of the subject before moving on to the tasks below: we suggest you paint a color wheel and identify primary, secondary, and tertiary colors. Also, try to understand complementary colors and terms such as hue, value, tone, saturation, tint, and harmony.

P = Primary colors:
red, yellow, and blue

S = Secondary colors:
orange, green, and purple/violet

T = Tertiary colors:
red-violet, violet-blue, blue-green, yellow-green, yellow-orange, red-orange

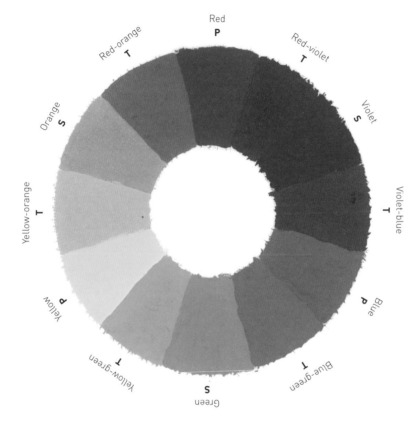

1 Experiment with mixing complementary color pairings (plus white) to create a series of subtle hues, grays, and neutral colors.

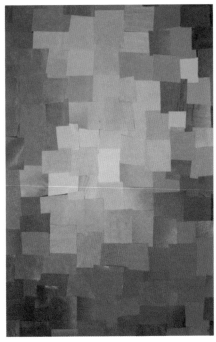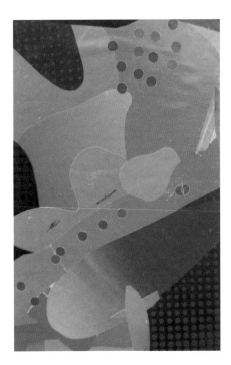

2 Complete a series of abstract compositions using colored paper cut from
magazines. Create compositions that are warm, cool, harmonious, or
complementary in their use of color. Experiment with different proportions
and arrangements of color, giving consideration to hue, value, and saturation.

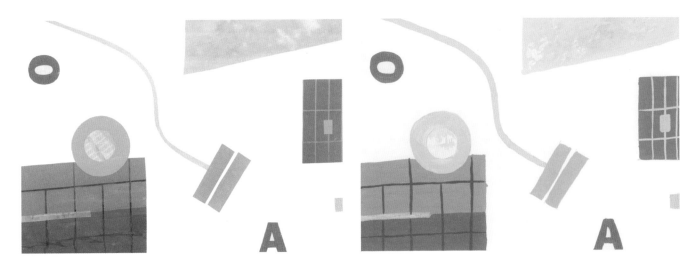

3 When you have completed a number of studies, select your preferred
composition and make a painted copy of the design. You will need to
experiment with your color mixing—we suggest you use gouache paint for
this exercise. Continue with your experiments. Reflect upon your work and
consider how you might apply the knowledge gained from these exercises to
your choice of color for an interior space.

Below and bottom
Both physical interaction and the tactile experience of space should be carefully considered by the designer.

Touch

...Hegel claimed that the only sense which can give a sensation of spatial depth is touch, because touch senses the weight, resistance, and three-dimensional shape (gestalt) of material bodies, and thus makes us aware that things extend away from us in all directions.

Vision reveals what the touch already knows. We could think of the sense of touch as the unconscious vision. Our eyes stroke distant surfaces, contours, and edges, and the unconscious tactile sensation determines the agreeableness or unpleasantness of the experience. The distant and the near are experienced with the same intensity, and they merge into one coherent experience.[11]

Through our sense of touch we record and interpret the built environment and we respond to the experience of touch physically, emotionally, and intellectually. This form of sensory perception is sometimes referred to as the "haptic system."

As designers, we can enhance and to some extent control this physical and psychological experience by considering, for example, the feel of a door handle or the weight of a door; the length of stride needed to climb steps; the relationship of our bodies to the height, width, and breadth of a room, which can liberate or oppress the body; the rhythm and "pace" of a space; the textures that affect our hands and feet; and the temperatures of objects that we touch.

Consciously or subconsciously, our bodies are in constant dialog with our material world, and the designer should make conscious decisions about the quality of that material world: textural juxtapositions and contrasts, the wall that is leaned upon, the floor that is sat upon, and the balustrade that is gripped.

11 Pallasmaa, op cit., p. 42.

Left and below

Philippe Rahm Architects work with temperature as a material: the hot and the cold, the heat and humidity of a place. In their pavilion, Digestible Gulf Stream, for the 2008 Venice Biennale, they explored the potential of these "materials": conventional boundaries of space (walls and doors) were abandoned, and space was defined using shifts of temperature to create thresholds and enclosure.

Bottom row

Nosigner is a Japanese artist and designer whose installations often emphasize a particular aspect of the multi-sensory nature of spatial experience. He creates ethereal, often monochromatic spaces using materials with subtly different textures and scales of opacity and translucency; he has explored the "haptic system" in his work. More than 20 people contributed to his exhibition, TECHTILE#3, at the K Gallery in Japan, a collective work that made visible the everyday surface textures that the conscious mind fails to perceive but that the body "remembers." Metal foil was used to create casts of the city's surfaces, which were assembled in the gallery: an immersion in, and a memory of, the tactile, textural, haptic experience of the city.

Smell and taste

How a space smells or "tastes" are unlikely to be a primary consideration for the designer when selecting materials. However, smell is a primordial sense and can act as a long-term memory aid; it can be very evocative and can remind us of a spatial experience that may have occurred many years earlier:

This page
In her proposal for the redesign of Portsmouth University's graduation ceremony, Fiona Damiano, a third-year student, designed a series of interventions, which included the use of flowers as a visual and olfactory signal to students and local residents that graduation and a period of academic celebration had begun. The scent of flowers is used to define a route and to mark the celebration of graduation.

In the home of his parents, which was one of the Grunderzeit bourgeois villas in the town, there was a wonderful parquet floor in the formal reception room, into which the children (including the young Hans-Georg) were not allowed to enter except on special occasions like Christmas. ... Gadamer spoke of this surface as something magical—a wonderful wooden floor, immaculately well-kept and polished so that it filled the space with the smell of wax.[12]

There are certain smells that we associate with different emotional states; incense in a church, baking bread, percolating coffee, or essential oils in a bathhouse all have the potential to engender a sense of well-being.

As infants, our sense of smell, taste, and oral sensations are used to construct our understanding of the world. All materials and objects are raised to the nose and mouth to explore: to sense smell, taste, and the tactile. As we grow and other senses develop, these instinctive behaviors become less important; however, they nevertheless remain powerful methods of reading and interpreting our environment:

There is a subtle transference between the tactile and taste experiences. Vision becomes transferred to taste as well; certain colors and delicate details evoke oral sensations. A delicately polished stone surface is subliminally sensed by the tongue.[13]

This quote suggests that in addition to material qualities such as texture, color can also provoke an oral response: the "taste" of red or blue.

The site of a new design intervention may well have an oral and an olfactory personality, existing materials such as metals, plastics, rubber, wood, varnish, and wax all omit particular odors and tastes: acrid, sour, sweet, salt, clear, etc. These smells and tastes have the potential to inform material choices for the new intervention, as the "inclusive" sensory system equates these senses with colors, tones, or textures.

12 Taylor and Preston, op. cit., p. 145.
13 Pallasmaa, op. cit., p. 59.

Hearing

The acoustic qualities of materials within a space can be manipulated to enhance the transmission or absorption of sound. Hard materials can be used to reflect sound and to create rooms that are acoustically "live" and resonant; such spaces may be uncomfortable for long periods of time (this is often cited as a problem in classrooms). Alternatively, perforated materials, fabrics, and carpets can be used to soften and absorb sound. Consider again the contrast between the luxurious restaurant where people are encouraged to linger and the local café—the quality of sound will be very different as a result of the materials selected for each:

Listen! Interiors are like large instruments, collecting sound, amplifying it, transmitting it elsewhere. That has to do with the shape peculiar to each room and with the surfaces of the materials they contain, and the way those materials have been applied.[14]

Materials can be selected to optimize the acoustic experience of a space relative to its function. For example, auditoriums have very particular acoustic requirements wherein form and materials are designed to reflect, project, and absorb speech, song, and music; when musicians speak of their favorite performance spaces they are usually referring to the acoustic qualities of the space. In other situations, such as a domestic interior or an office, it may be necessary to provide "acoustic separation," whereby materials are used to absorb and contain sound in order to maintain privacy. Acoustic engineers (acousticians) understand the science of sound, and can advise about appropriate material specification.

Austrian artist Bernhard Leitner (born 1938) is a pioneer of sound installations. His sound–space sculptures (or architectural soundscapes) use sound to attract and direct, to define space, and to caress and envelop the user; sound is not just heard but is experienced viscerally. Edwin van der Heide (Dutch, born 1970) is also an artist and researcher interested in the qualities of sound. In his "sound work" *Son-O-House* in the Netherlands, materials and form are used to create a space in which the visitor is both audience and composer: sensors detect the movement of visitors and translate it into a musical score and performance. This metallic structure has an organic form that reflects the dynamic nature of the space: a shifting musical landscape.

This form of artistic endeavor and research has resonance for the designer. As stated, material choices have pragmatic implications when considering the acoustic quality of a space, but, as these artworks demonstrate, sound is more than just an aural experience.

A considered response to the sensory qualities of materials will benefit all users of an interior but could also improve the inclusivity of a space. For example, the use of tactile surfaces at significant thresholds or hardware that contrasts visually with the material of a door could improve the experience of people with visual impairments; the acoustic properties of materials could enhance or impair the interior experience for those with poor hearing or a disability such as autism; the width of corridors and ramps and the associated floor finishes could ease or hinder access for people using wheelchairs or pushing strollers.

In discussing the sensory properties of materials, we referred to the sense of life/comfort. This sense allows us to respond to our environment and perceive what is good or bad for our well-being. The next section illustrates how the environmental properties of materials have a direct relationship to our individual and collective well-being.

14 Zumthor, op. cit., p. 29.

Left and far left
Edwin van der Heide's sound installation, *Son-O-House*, emphasizes the relationship between spatial experience and our aural sense.

Opposite
An interpretation of Desso Carpets' Cradle-to-Cradle diagram: a cycle of production that is eco-effective and adopts a "cradle to cradle" approach to manufacturing and consumption.

Environmental properties

With new technologies and brute force energy supplies (such as fossil fuels), the Industrial Revolution gave humans unprecedented power over nature. No longer were people so dependent on natural forces, or so helpless against the vicissitudes of land and sea. They could override nature to accomplish their goals as never before. But in the process a massive disconnection has taken place.[15]

Since the Industrial Revolution, suppliers and producers of materials have focused on economic growth while neglecting the broader issues and responsibilities of the manufacturing process. Complicit consumers (including the designer as specifier) have bought goods, welcomed cheaper products with little regard for the people who manufacture them, and accepted the associated waste as an inevitable consequence of "progress" and development. In addition, the toxic content of many materials and products is now known to cause higher than foreseen levels of asthma, allergy, birth defects, genetic mutations, and cancer.

As a consequence, natural, finite resources have been depleted, the global atmosphere and environment is polluted, and animal and human well-being (physical and emotional) has been compromised.

So here is a problem for the designer: a problem with no "quick fix" solution and no easy answers, a problem that can overwhelm and depress and leave the individual feeling helpless and ineffectual. However, it is also a problem that can inspire creativity and a commitment to change: many individuals understand that their actions matter, and they have brought about a paradigm shift that is transforming patterns of production and consumption.

Designers have influence and responsibilities, and through the choices they make they can drive this paradigm shift and be part of the vision for a sustainable future. The issues are complex and there are no straightforward "answers," but there are strategies that can be adopted that will make a difference: be informed, be responsible, be creative.

Be informed

There are many books that will inform and inspire you about the broad agenda of sustainability, and specifically its relation to materials. One of the most influential books of our generation is Michael Braungart and William McDonough's *Cradle to Cradle*, first published in 2002.

In this text, Braungart and McDonough challenge the "three Rs" mantra—Reduce, Reuse, Recycle—and the associated aspiration to become eco-efficient. They claim that simply reducing our consumption of natural resources, toxins, and production of waste and becoming more efficient does not ultimately change anything; it simply slows the process of denuding resources and degrading the environment, and as the impact is slower it becomes harder to detect and therefore appears to be acceptable. They also claim that the process of recycling is actually a process of "down-cycling," wherein materials are reused but through this process become contaminated and ultimately discarded as waste.

Instead, Braungart and McDonough propose a "cradle to cradle" approach to manufacturing and use, a process that is eco-effective rather than eco-efficient. They define

15 Michael Braungart and William McDonough, *Cradle to Cradle: Remaking the way we make things*, Vintage, 2009, p. 128.

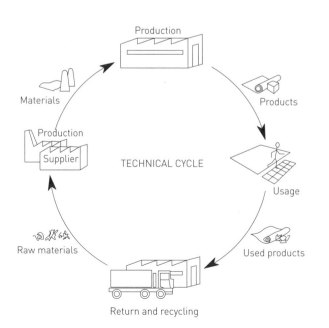

TECHNICAL CYCLE

Materials — Production — Products — Usage — Used products — Return and recycling — Raw materials — Production Supplier

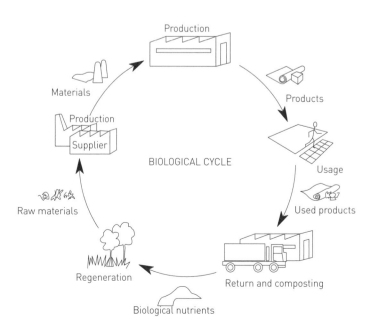

BIOLOGICAL CYCLE

Materials — Production — Products — Usage — Used products — Return and composting — Biological nutrients — Regeneration — Raw materials — Production Supplier

two types of material: X (biological materials) and Y (technical materials) and claim that if these substances can remain isolated in separate cycles (even if they are used within the same product or composite material), they can avoid contamination and can be reused endlessly; they refer to this process as "up-cycling."

Desso, a manufacturer of carpets, serves as one example of a company that has adopted the "cradle to cradle" philosophy: it is manufacturing products with materials that can be "up-cycled." The manufacturing processes minimize use of water and energy and avoid use of toxins—these are replaced by chemicals that can have positive benefits for health and the environment. All the materials used in the carpets can be extracted and reused in an endless cycle of production.

When assessing the environmental properties of materials for selection, critical and analytical skills must be used to interrogate manufacturers. It cannot be assumed that a material that carries a "green" label is truly environmentally friendly; at its most cynical, green branding promotes consumerism and waste.

Information and advice can be sought from an increasing number of sources such as online databases and websites, specialist libraries of materials, journals, agencies, and institutions, guides to specifying materials, and a plethora of books about the subject—some of these sources are listed at the back of this book. Often, clients will also appoint sustainability or environmental consultants as part of the design team, trusted specialists who can provide reliable and current advice about materials specification.

When working on existing buildings, there are opportunities to preserve, conserve, or restore existing materials, approaches which represent different values and philosophies of design and intervention. It is also important to be mindful that in an old building some materials, such as asbestos, may be toxic and will need to be removed or encapsulated.

In practice it is likely that the designer will be involved in decisions having an impact on the environment that go beyond materials and product specification—for example, ventilation and insulation, lighting design, and mechanical and electrical installations. These subjects do not form part of the focus of this book, but it is worth noting that designers will need to develop their understanding of these topics and contribute to any debate about them with clients and other consultants.

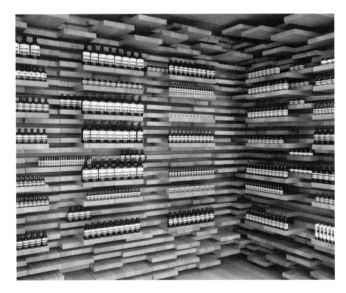

Above

In its design for the Aesop skincare store in rue Saint-Honoré in Paris, March Studios used only one material: Victorian Ash, a timber grown in renewable forests in Australia. To create this Jenga-like interior, 3,500 pieces of wood were hand cut and finished before being numbered according to complex detail drawings and loaded into shipping containers.

Above right

For the Padova Cratehouse, Padua, Italy, German artists Wolfgang Winter and Berthold Hörbelt constructed walls from re-appropriated plastic bottle crates, which provide color and form while allowing light to permeate the space—an innovative approach to minimizing and reusing material waste.

Be responsible

Eco-effective designers expand their vision from the primary purpose of a product or system and consider the whole. What are its goals and potential effects, both immediate and wide-ranging, with respect to both time and place? What is the entire system— cultural, commercial, ecological—of which this made thing, and way of making things, will be a part?[16]

It is essential for designers to be informed about the environmental agenda so that they are able to make responsible judgments about the issues associated with material selection. There are some simple principles that can be applied to the decision making, such as identifying and avoiding toxic, unhealthy materials, chemicals, and surface treatments. Braungart and McDonough refer to an "X" list that includes substances such as asbestos, benzene, vinyl chloride, antimony trioxide, and chromium, which are known to be teratogenic, mutagenic, or carcinogenic.

In the *Green Guide to the Architect's Job Book*, Sandy Halliday recommends that the designer should:

Vet the specification against a list of deleterious materials, considering the overall effect on the ability to source locally, indoor air quality, any implications for ventilation strategies, and the durability of wearing surfaces.[17]

There are also increasing numbers of guidelines, assessment tools (used to audit materials and assess their performance in terms of manufacturing processes, life cycle, longevity, and maintenance), and regulatory bodies that ensure that designers and clients adopt good practice and take a responsible attitude toward environmental issues.

The Leadership of Energy and Environmental Design (LEED) is the United States Green Building Council's (USGBC) points rating system for buildings that adhere to a green footprint. The rating system is designed to reward buildings that take into account the environment and the health of the users. LEED points or credits are weighted to reflect their impact on the environment. The system offers four certification levels: certified, silver, gold, and platinum (the highest honor). Certification is regulated by the independent, non-profit Green Building Certification Institute (GBCI). A building must fulfill the designated prerequisites and earn a minimum amount of points for certification. Many types of structure can be LEED-certified, such as commercial interiors, core and shell, new construction, schools, healthcare, retail, and residential. LEED-certified buildings address sustainability in these key areas:

- Sustainable sites
- Water efficiency
- Energy and atmosphere
- Materials and resources
- Indoor environmental quality
- Locations and linkages
- Awareness and education
- Innovation in design
- Regional priority

Regulatory bodies outside the US include:

DGNB German Society for Sustainable Building
MINERGIE Swiss Sustainable Building Standard
HQE French tool for rating and implementing green building solutions
EU Green Building Program European Commission's green building program for non-residential buildings.
CASBEE Japanese tool for assessing and rating the environmental performance of buildings
BREEAM British rating system and tool for environmental assessment
The Code for Sustainable Homes British standard for rating and assessing new homes

When considering alternative products for an interior the design team will also face dilemmas associated with cost and choice: the product or material that is preferred for ethical reasons may also cost more and there may be alternatives that are aesthetically more desirable. It might also be difficult to determine which products are the most sustainable as you try to balance issues associated with source, transportation, manufacturing processes, human welfare, toxicity, etc.

In addition to ensuring that materials are "eco-effective," it is also important to be aware of the standard sizes of materials such as plywood and sheet metals. Waste ought to be minimized by using modules that correspond with the standard dimensions, and consideration needs to be given to how the leftover pieces, or "offcuts," could be used. Some materials and products for interiors work have also been designed using only waste material.

The transition to an eco-effective future will take time, but the designer can help to realize that vision by approaching the process of selecting materials and products with a sound set of guiding principles and creative thinking.

16 Ibid., p. 82.
17 Sandy Halliday, *Green Guide to the Architect's Job Book*, London: RIBA Publishing, 2000, p. 19.

Below left
The eco-efficiency strategy has been used to great effect in the work of Dutch designer Piet Hein Eek in his product "99% Cabinets." Working within the dimensions of Cor-ten sheet steel, modular shelves have been designed that reduce material waste/offcuts to less than 1 percent. The aim of minimizing the use of materials has also been applied to packaging processes, wherein offcuts of wood from the studio are used to protect the shelves in transit.

Below
Tejo Remy of Droog Design created this chair design using old textiles; the chairs can be personalized using the user's own materials—a way of retaining memories associated with old, familiar garments.

Left
Smile Plastics were originally created from recycled domestic plastic bottles; they now also use old Wellington boots, cell phones, and CDs. At Langley Green Hospital, Crawley, UK, David Watson Works have designed and made a striking bench using strips of plastic offcuts from Smile Plastics.

TIP ANALYZING SUSTAINABILITY

Ensuring that your practice as a designer is ethical and sustainable can be very challenging. This exercise provides an opportunity to explore the issues associated with materials and their impact on the environment:

- Select a material or product that you are proposing to use in one of your projects; for example, wood, as illustrated in this proposal for a café in Japan by Design Spirits.

- Assess the environmental credentials of the material. Consider: where and by whom it is made; transportation; raw materials; management of material sources; toxicity; potential for reuse; use of fixings, adhesives, and finishes. The diagram below examines the impact of using wood in an interior.

- Define the negative and positive environmental attributes of this material.

- Repeat the exercise with an alternative material, perhaps a different type or supplier of wood or a completely different material such as a polymer.

- Identify which of the materials or products has the least detrimental effect on the environment. Consider whether there are any other, more sustainable, alternatives.

Assessing the environmental impact of wood

Timber will be sawn into set sizes and shapes; does your design make the most of these basic sizes?
This process uses electricity, and in turn produces greenhouse gases.

The timber might then end up at a supplier. This could be another leg in the journey from the forest to the project site.

What is the product's lifespan? Can it be recycled or reused afterward? How much energy does it take to be recycled into another product or form?

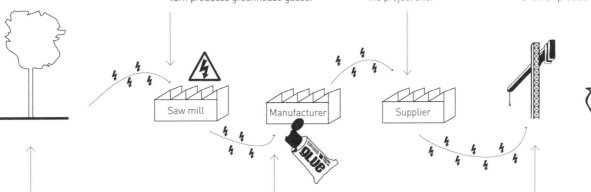

Timber can be obtained from various sources; here are some points to consider:
- Is its growth sustainable?
- How well managed are the forests concerned?
- How quickly are trees grown and replaced?
- How far away is the timber grown; will the journey to site be 50 miles or 5,000 miles?

Some timber will be engineered or manufactured. This process could involve bleaches, solvents, or substances such as formaldehyde. These are harmful to the environment in terms of their own production and their subsequent use.

Eventually the timber product arrives at site. How much wastage will there be? What extra materials and energy are required to install the material?

Be creative

While critical thinking and ethics can be applied to the selection and specification of conventional products and materials, creative thinking can also be used to achieve sustainable and innovative interiors.

Many contemporary practitioners have been inspired by the sustainability agenda to design in an inventive way, reusing and re-appropriating existing materials to create a twenty-first-century "hybrid" aesthetic. These designs, often for small one-off interiors or products, have in common their use of the found object or the assembly of an eclectic range of discarded materials that are brought together to create a new cohesive whole. This new approach to design has emerged in response to the green agenda, but also borrows from the much more established practices of "outsider artists" and the Surrealists. In 1917 the French Surrealist Marcel Duchamp (1887–1968) exhibited *Fountain*, which he referred to as a "readymade"—a term he used for an artwork that re-presented and repositioned standard, manufactured goods in the context of the gallery.

The French outsider artist Ferdinand Cheval (1836–1924) spent three decades building a palace made from the stones he collected on his daily postal route, creating a unique material folly. Similarly, in 1968 American retiree John Milkovisch began work on his "Beer Can House" using flattened cans to clad and insulate his home, and ring pulls and can lids to create decorative screens and blinds. Many other people have applied similar approaches to creating buildings, interiors, and furniture, including Piet Hein Eek, Most Architecture, Ron Arad, Michael Marriott, and Droog Design.

Right and below right
John Milkovisch's Beer Can House in Houston, Texas.

Left and far left
Piet Hein Eek, the designer of "99% Cabinets," illustrated on page 84, also creates new furniture using scraps of materials and discarded objects, and composes them to create elegant new forms that sensitively respond to the properties of the original: a poetic, harmonious assembly of color, texture, and form.

Right
Michael Marriott's "Four Drawers" unit is constructed from birch plywood, pegboard, and discarded Spanish fruit crates.

Above and right
Using a similar approach to re-appropriation as Eek, the Dutch practice Most Architecture has designed a temporary office for the Amsterdam advertising agency Brand Base. The client was keen for the designers to adopt a sustainable approach to the use of materials—which resulted in the final assembly of industrial palettes, configured to invite the user to sit, meet, lean, or lie on the surfaces.

Subjective properties

In addition to empirical, physical properties, materials may also have subjective attributes that emanate from a person's experience and emotional response or that arise from social, political, or culturally constructed readings of them.

When selecting materials for an interior, the designer needs to think beyond the very basic requirements (the physical properties of a material) and consider their subjective properties and the alternative readings they might suggest. Within product and industrial design, textiles, furniture, and lighting design, this might relate to "product personality." Product personality is not just to do with the form and appearance of materials, but also the sensory experience—how much the materials weigh, whether they are cool to the touch, their smell and taste, and the cultural and contextual associations. So for example, we equate plastic with cheap toys, gold with wealth, and fine jewelry and wood with craftsmanship and a sense of tradition. Materials are imbued with these meanings, and it is important to understand the alternative readings and connotations that can inform a spatial concept.

Personal readings

Materials can evoke memories in the individual that may have a particular resonance for that person while holding little significance for others; this can often be the case when responding to their sensory nature. For example, a certain material smell, sound, or texture could instantly trigger memories of a particular time or place from the past—the material allows us to remember. It is also possible for us to have memories of materials themselves because they had a particular ambience or atmosphere that we might associate with feelings of numinous happiness or reflection—a sense of place that creates a feeling of well-being.

Socially or politically constructed readings

Identities (status, gender, ethnicity, etc.) can also be expressed, reinforced, or defined by materials. Consider the objects and furnishings that surround us in our homes, or the material quality of a housing estate, a youth club, a jazz club, a municipal building, or a stately home—buildings that have different meanings and associations for different people but that are defined, in part, by their materials.

Materials can also be imbued with meaning that is socially constructed and can be used to symbolize hierarchy, power, and status. Compare, for example, a flight of metal stairs and a flight of stone stairs. Where do you imagine each set of stairs leads? With what kind of building might they be associated? Does your immediate response suggest that you have any preconstructed reading of these materials?

Materials have often been used to express status and wealth. Stone is an expensive material that requires considerable skill to work effectively, and in Europe it has become symbolic of power, wealth, and prestige. Exposed brick structures have been used in some places to create elaborate monuments, stately buildings, cathedrals, and mosques; however, in parts of Europe they were often faced with stone, or a plaster surface carefully painted to resemble stone, in order to elevate the status of the building.

Cultural readings

Materials can also have local readings that respond to religious and cultural traditions, or to the conventions of building and craft. In Islamic art and architecture, mosaic tiles colored using local pigments were arranged to create complex geometric patterns symbolizing unity and order—figurative art was avoided, and imperfections were built into the designs as a recognition of the supremacy of God; only God is perfect.

Another type of surface or decorative technique is that of *sgrafitto*, wherein a plaster or ceramic surface is scratched in order to create giant drawings on building façades, to create frescoes, or to decorate artifacts. These local traditional techniques, seen in European and African art, have been borrowed and developed by designers to contribute toward an evolving language of materials.

In Japan, family-based guilds of carpenters were established, and they developed secret methods of constructing and crafting timber. Some of the guilds specialized in domestic properties and storehouses, others in the construction of temples and the famous Shinto shrines. Each guild applied different levels of refinement and methods of detailing to its timber constructions. Japanese carpenters also had to deal with local issues such as earthquakes, so timber joints were designed to be flexible and to allow some movement.

Above, left to right
Traditions and cultural differences can be observed in the use of patterns, colors, and materials. These examples are found in Morocco and Spain.

Left
The crafted timber of a traditional Japanese house.

The maker's reading

The "dynamic of material" is a term used to express how we understand that a material should be used in art and design. The Finnish craftsman Tapio Wirkkala (1915–1985) explains that "all materials have their own unwritten laws. This is forgotten far too often. You should never be violent with a material you're working on, and the designer should aim at being in harmony with his material."[18]

The idea of a designer "making," rather than just designing, suggests that he or she should have an understanding of materials that parallel the understanding a sculptor might have of stone or wood: an intimate knowledge of the material's potential allows form to emerge. For the sculptor, materials are the substance of art—a ball of clay can become many things, but has limitations that the sculptor understands; for the designer, materials are the substance of place making and the designer must have the same understanding of their material palette, i.e. the potential and limitations of materials:

You cannot make what you want to make, but what the material permits you to make. You cannot make out of marble what you would make out of wood, or out of wood what you would make out of stone ... each material has its own life.[19]

By definition, these alternative and subjective readings of materials can be difficult for designers to navigate. However, it is important for them to consider the possible interpretations of material configurations, as this can result in more sensitive designs, creative interpretations, conceptual depth, and integrity.

When considering the properties of a material and how one material relates to others in a palette, the designer will also consider how materials are to be assembled and constructed. He or she will resolve material interfaces and intersections, joints, junctions, fixings, and fastenings. This aspect of design could occur at any stage of a project, and is sometimes referred to as "detail" or "detailing." We shall explore the concept and process of detailing in the next section.

18 http://www.scandinaviandesign.com/tapioWirkkala/index1.htm
(accessed 12.12.11)
19 Dorothy Dudley, "Brancusi," *Dial*, 82, February 1927, p. 124.

9. Material detail

We have a rule that says sometimes the detail wags the dog. You don't necessarily go from the general to the particular, but rather often you do the detail at the beginning very much to inform.[20]

Material detail, or detailing, is the process by which the designer resolves material interfaces, assembly, and construction.

Detailing is often viewed as a process that occurs at the latter stages of a project; however, spatial concepts can be derived from a material detail, or details can be developed as the materials palette is selected; it is not a procedural, linear process.

Czech-born architect Eva Jiricna (born 1939) has indicated that her design process is very much a matter of beginning with what others would conventionally regard as detail. She likes to begin by choosing materials and drawing full-size details of their junctions:

In our office we usually start with full-size detail … if we have for example, some ideas of what we are going to create with different junctions, then we can create a layout which would be good because certain materials only join in a certain way comfortably.[21]

20 Robert Venturi quoted in Bryan Lawson, *How Designers Think*, Architectural Press, 2009, p. 39.
21 Eva Jiricna quoted in ibid., p. 39.

Left
Beginning with an understanding of glass and how it is detailed and assembled has informed Eva Jiricna's design of the whole interior at the Boodles flagship jewelry store in London.

Below, left to right
At the Castelvecchio Museum,
Carlo Scarpa made clear
demarcations between new and
existing materials.

Material detailing or assembly should be an intrinsic part of
an interior design process and material details should relate
to the overall concept, creating a cohesive relationship
between the macro and micro. For example, in the context
of an existing building it might be the designer's intention
to make a clear demarcation between the old and the new.
The approach to detailing will reflect this concept in an
expression of "separation": the worn quality of existing
materials might be juxtaposed with new materials; new
materials might always appear to "float" above the old, or
old and new might be separated by "negative details" or
shadow gaps.

Material details might also express a particular
philosophy or movement of architecture and design—
concepts that suggest a consistent approach to all aspects
of design in each context (Modernism is a good example
of this). For example, all methods of fixing and fastening
materials might be exposed (a concept of "truthfulness")
or, alternatively, many aspects of an interior's physical
manifestation could be hidden, creating, for example, the
impression of floating surfaces (a concept of "illusion").

When resolving material interfaces and assembling
materials, designers can apply tried and tested
construction methods and they can also specify factory
finished, prefabricated details that are designed by the
manufacturer or supplier of a particular product, for
example acoustic paneling or partitioning systems.

In the past, material details and assembly methods
would have been resolved by artisans and craftspeople.
They would apply the techniques and design vocabulary
of their particular trade: the stonemason, the language
of stone; the carpenter, the language of wood; the
blacksmith, the language of iron and steel; or the glazier,
the language of glass.

Left and below left
Material details observed in Venice.

The traditional techniques used and the physicality of these crafts gave historical buildings their integrity, and are qualities that people often seek in handmade products today: the mark of the maker, impressions left by hands and tools that could not be replicated by machine, the unique and the "honest."

Craft traditions have their appeal and important contributions to make to the quality of an interior; however, good-quality modern detailing can also have integrity. The contemporary designer has access to sophisticated materials and manufacturing processes when resolving how materials are to be detailed and assembled. The alignment of new materials technologies, computer-aided design (CAD) and computer-aided manufacturing (CAM), has also presented new possibilities for the innovative designer; spaces that could previously only

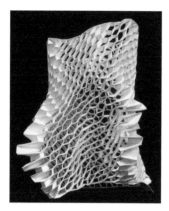

Above and below
Andrew Kudless of US design
studio Matsys completed the
Manifold installation as part of
a research project at London's
Architectural Association in
2004. As a form of biomimetic
design, *Manifold* makes reference
to honeycomb structures.
Using both digital and physical
prototyping, the final element
of the installation, "Honeycomb
Morphologies," was constructed
from a series of cardboard cells,
each varying in their form, size,
shape, and orientation.

be imagined can now be realized. Traditional functions,
processes, and vocabularies of materials are being
challenged by these new technologies; blocks and sheet
materials (traditional building components) are coupled
with polymorphous, fluid substances and natural materials
juxtaposed with the synthetic.

*By now functional substitutes for virtually all organic
and natural materials have been found in the shape of
plastic and polymorphous substances: wool, cotton,
silk, and linen are thus all susceptible of replacement
by nylon and its countless variants, while wood, stone,
and metal are giving way to concrete and polystyrene.*[22]

*… the manufacture of synthetics means that
materials lose their symbolic naturalness and become
polymorphous, so achieving a higher degree of
abstractness which makes possible a universal play
of associations among materials, and hence too a
transcendence of the formal antithesis between natural
and artificial materials.*[23]

22 Jean Baudrillard, quoted in Taylor and Preston, op. cit., p. 40.
23 Ibid.

These new "crafts" and technical processes are generating new aesthetics, complex organic forms, and a resurgence of the decorative: a new "Rococo."

Matsys is a design studio concerned with the relationships between different areas of engineering, biology, and computation; they consider that architecture can

be understood as a material body with its own intrinsic and extrinsic forces relating to form, growth, and behavior; the studio investigates methodologies of performative integration through geometric and material differentiation.[24]

24 http://matsysdesign.com/category/information/
   profile/ (accessed 04.07.11).

Above and below
Working in collaboration with Rob Henderson and Studio Lynn, Brennan Buck created the installation *Technicolor Bloom*. First exhibited in Vienna in 2008, it is a spatial study of both the "literal and phenomenological effects of three-dimensional pattern." Using digital design and manufacturing processes, 1,400 flat plywood panels were connected to create complex double curves and filigree patterns.

Below and bottom
"Tiles" is a system designed by Studio Bouroullec for the Kvadrat showroom in Stockholm. The individual thermocompressed foam and fabric tiles can be connected using double-injected rubber bands and a slot detail; the tiles can be connected and disconnected to create flexible partitions of space.

In his collaboration with Elbo Group and Studio Lynn, Brennan Buck has utilized simple digital design and manufacturing processes to create complex form and pattern:

Built from 1400 uniquely cut, flat plywood panels, the installation favors intense detail over seamless elegance. At the same time, it proliferates continuity: continuity of surface morphology, continuity of the structural patterns across those surfaces, and varied interrelationships of depth and color from one surface to the next.[25]

It is clear that detailing can be an imaginative process, an opportunity to apply inventive solutions to the minutiae of detail at the micro as well as the macro scale. In their projects for Kvadrat showrooms, designers Ronan and Erwan Bouroullec have created dynamic forms using repeat components made from fabric, which are folded and joined using various ingenious techniques. These design and detailing methodologies borrow from and subvert architectural geometries (the geodesic dome) and the language of textiles.

25 http://www.technicolorbloom.com/ (accessed 04.07.11).

Designers can also look to nature when trying to solve problems of detail, a process called "biomimicry." Biomimicry encourages a respect for and an emulation of "forms, processes, systems, and strategies" found in nature.[26] For example, designers and scientists have developed carbon-absorbing cements following their observations of coral, skeletal structures to support building membranes, and Velcro inspired by the form of the burr.

26 http://www.asknature.org/article/view/what_ is_biomimicry (accessed 04.07.11).

Above
Studio Bouroullec also designed Kvadrat's showroom in Copenhagen. In this installation, similar tiles are connected to form "Clouds," a suspended, motorized fabric partition.

Below
Artist and designer Rachel O'Neill looks to the natural world for inspiration when designing and detailing products—a process referred to as biomimicry or biomorphic design. "Nest," pictured, is a textural lighting design made from dyed Velcro and goose feathers wrapped around an aluminum frame.

Below and bottom
In collaboration with Werkplaats
de Rijk/Parthesius, Panelite,
and RAM Contract, OMA
created a new material—"Prada
Sponge"—used at the Prada
store in Los Angeles. The
material emerged from
development that began with
a backlit cleaning sponge.
The team experimented with
milling and casting techniques,
and three-dimensional computer
modeling was used to translate
the handcrafted prototype
into the final product: a new
polyurethane composite.

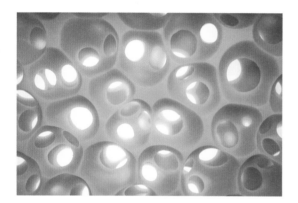

Although there are fewer artisans and craftspeople
involved in the construction of contemporary buildings
than in historical structures, the designer and the client
can refer to specialist suppliers and contractors for advice
about construction methods and material details. This is
particularly useful if the designer is working on a non-
standard design—a "one-off." In this case, the relationship
between the designer and the specialist contractor can be
very fruitful. Contractors can offer the expert knowledge
about a particular material or method of construction
and they have the facilities to manufacture prototypes
and test alternatives, which can then be viewed by the
designer and the client. Prototypes can be used to resolve
aesthetic decisions, construction methods, and technical
performance such as acoustics or light emissions.

It is important that the contractor's or manufacturer's
knowledge is valued by the designer. The manufacturer
understands the physical properties of the materials, how
they can be fixed, and the potential for their application in
different situations. Suppliers and contractors can advise
about material finishes and surface treatments, and other
essential aspects of material detailing:

TIP KEEP A VISUAL DIARY

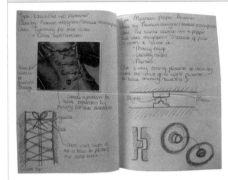 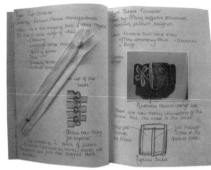 

These images are taken from a diary of fixings and fastenings kept by a student. By recording a wide range of different methods of fixing and fastening materials, designers can expand their understanding and develop an innovative language of material detailing that can be applied to interiors.

The process of finishing, of dressing, cutting, polishing, curing, sealing, and so on, can modify the visual appearance of materials every bit as much as any opaque coating. In practice, materials like wood, stone, brick, metal, and leather grown or produced through natural processes are valued as such when their finishes enhance or at least do not obscure the complexity, depth, or variety of their appearance.[27]

The language of material finishes and coatings is poetic and can evoke particular material atmospheres and sensory responses, consider: waxed, oiled, riven, honed, glazed, polished, satin-polished, varnished, lacquered, etc. These words suggest particular smells, sounds, and textures that can be manipulated by the designer.

Examples of material detail drawings and on-site construction are included in the case studies in Part VI. There are also many books and periodicals that provide examples of detailing and construction methods for specific materials. Some of these are listed in the further reading section at the end of the book.

27 Taylor and Preston, op. cit., p. 58.

STEP BY STEP REPEAT COMPONENTS

It is important for the creative designer to look beyond obvious solutions for materials application and detailing. Playing with and testing alternatives can lead to innovative and unpredictable solutions for a simple partition.

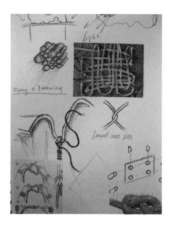  

1 Maintain a visual diary to record alternative methods of fixing, fastening, and joining materials. Aim to look beyond (although do include) architectural methods, to gain a broader understanding of materials and details. Include drawings, photographs, and images.

2 Using only cotton and paper, experiment with making alternative repeat components and methods of fixing and fastening.

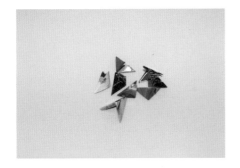
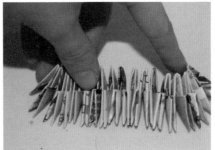
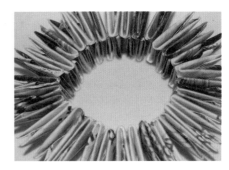

3 Select one of your designs and consider alternative ways of assembling your repeat components.

4 Using your repeat component or product, design a "partition of space." Give careful thought to the material quality of the component and its appearance when repeated as well as to any fixings and fastenings: these should be an integral part of your design not an afterthought (avoid using any adhesives or tape). Issues of opacity, translucency, solid, and void, and issues of surface, form, color, and texture should also be considered. Identify alternative applications for your design.

STEP BY STEP RECORDING JOINTS AND JUNCTIONS

An interior space can be characterized or defined by its material joints and junctions. These range from the literal joints created by structures to joints and junctions created by planes and the intersection of materials, and finally the fastenings and fixings that "dress" the space. This exercise encourages an ongoing study of these three-dimensional interfaces. This example is based upon the Aspex Gallery in Portsmouth, England.

1 Begin a visual diary in which you can record your observations of joints and junctions. Identify the space or place you wish to explore, and begin by recording photographically.

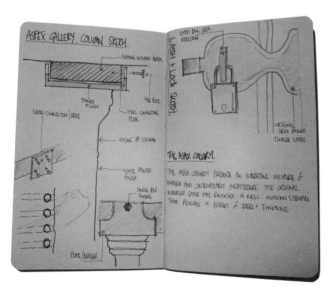

2 Think about the largest scales first. Identify and observe the structure of the building if possible, photograph and sketch its joints and connections—think about how these connections work and the combination of materials used in them. These large joints and junctions can be recorded in the form of quick, sectional sketches.

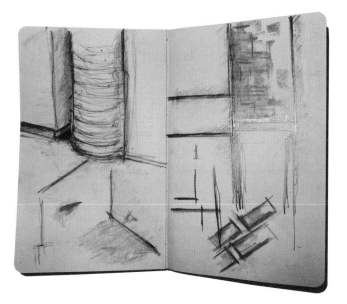

3 Identify and observe the junctions and joins between materials within the space; observe and sketch the edges and shadows that are formed when materials converge. Think about how these materials connect to each other in terms of fixings, fastenings, and layers—are there any unifying principles that determine how these materials meet, intersect, and connect?

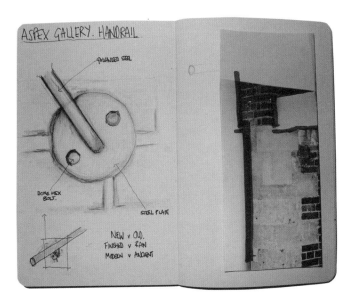

4 Finally, identify the joints and junctions of the fixings and fastenings within the space; record the material qualities and how people interact with them. This example shows a detailed study of how a new handrail connects to the existing brickwork of the building.

STEP BY STEP VISITING AN EXEMPLAR BUILDING

When visiting an exemplar building—in this case Carlo Scarpa's Querini Stampalia foundation in Venice—it is good practice to analyze the designer's use of materials and record your observations. This can be done using drawings, notes, and photographs. This Step by Step uses photographs.

Materials at the scale of the room:
Polished plaster ceiling
Stone walls
Concrete floor
External glazing

1 Begin by making a record of the whole space. This could take the form of sketches or photographs of the room and notes that record the materials used at the scale of the room.

The stone wall panels have a very distinctive pitted surface, which suggests the stone is travertine. The stone panels are divided with horizontal brass strips from which paintings can be hung. The wall is punctuated with vertical, flush glass light fittings. The concrete is embedded with tiny stones, and is articulated with stone or concrete strips. These are integrated at irregular but harmonic intervals ... like musical notes.

2 Now take a closer look at these finishes and record your analytical observations. Are there other materials that you can see at this scale? Can you observe how materials are composed: fixings and fastenings, etc.?

3 Now focus on a particular feature of the room—for example, a piece of built-in furniture, a light fitting, or a door. Examine material junctions and composition.

The stone door is framed with a flush brass strip fixed with countersunk brass screws. The hinge is made of steel or iron, and is offset so that the door is flush with the wall when closed. There is an adjacent wall clad with brass—it has a dull patina but begins to reflect the color of the red polished-plaster ceiling.

4 Look more closely at the feature you have identified. Can you observe any new materials? What is the function of the new material?

PART IV COMMUNICATING FROM CONCEPT TO COMPLETION

I don't make a big myth out of drawings. A real representation of something would destroy it. The best images of something not yet built are the ones that give you a broad open feeling, like a promise. ... You have to spread some enthusiasm for a project before it is built. You have to do it for yourself and to contaminate other people.[1]

To design is to imagine, and the imagined interior requires many different forms of illustration, expression, representation, and communication to convey its concepts, substance, and materiality; from this process of drawing and writing, the realized interior will emerge.

It is these themes that will be explored in this section of the book. Some of the methods of communicating material thinking will be visually exploratory and experimental; others, more precise presentations of the imagined interior. The processes will include drawings and models and also written documents, or a combination of both approaches. These alternative representations of materials need to be used in order to stimulate the imagination and to allow a shared understanding of design intentions.

Before designers begin to communicate their spatial ideas and use of materials, they must consider the purpose of the drawing or writing and what is to be conveyed by it. This will usually vary according to the project type, stage, and the intended "audience" for the documentation. For clarity we will refer to different stages of a project in order to explore the alternative communication methods used, but we will begin by considering the more general process of thinking and communication through drawing.

1 Peter Zumthor, lecture, Royal Academy, London Summerworks, 2006.

Below
This CAD visualization describes the material qualities of an interior.

Opposite
This drawing by Anne-Laure Carruth uses photography and Photoshop to describe the imagined interior of a seed bank project.

10. Thinking and communicating through drawing

The material qualities of an imagined interior—textures, form, color, pattern, and composition—can be described by making marks on paper, using models and samples, or by creating a virtual environment using CAD, all processes used to create representations and presentations of a spatial design.

A drawing in its broadest sense is simply a mark made with some purpose. More complex drawings can be about observing, gathering, thinking, and communicating information with varying degrees of expression, precision, and detail. Drawings can also move beyond two dimensions to take the form of collections of materials and objects—three-dimensional collages or "sketches" that could suggest spatial possibilities. Drawings can be used to analyze, to experiment, to explore concepts, and to develop ideas—a recorded thinking process.

Since the Renaissance drawing has been the primary method used to design and represent space. Conventions have been developed in which drawings have been combined with text and symbols to support the process of designing and constructing a space (consider plans, sections, elevations, lineweights, hatching, etc.).

In practice, drawings and models are used as tools to convey information and ideas to other designers, consultants, clients, and contractors, each of whom have different areas of expertise and differing objectives for the design project. Drawings (and models) can become a focal point for team conversations, discussions, and debates; information can be added and subtracted, problems identified and solved, and refinements agreed.

Although drawing is central to the design process, drawn notations have their limitations: they might hint at material qualities or properties, but they cannot always capture the phenomenology of materials. As Robin Evans points out in his essay "Translations from Drawing to Building," earth art, performance, installations, and environments that deal with architectural themes and space could not all be developed and communicated through the medium of drawing.[2] For example, he claims, if an installation by James Turrell was presented through plan and section, the drawings would indicate a design of "witless simplicity"—they would not capture the holistic spatial experiences that are created by manipulating our perceptions of space, materials, color and light: "Not all things architectural can be arrived at through drawing."

The tools we use within a studio—the computer, ink pen, mechanical pencil, tracing paper, cardboard, utility knife, etc.—all inform design production and possibly influence the material manifestation and character of the spaces we design. Over the last 30 years, technology—specifically computer-aided design (CAD)—has had a radical impact on drawing and design processes. Computer drawing is less physical than freehand drawing and perhaps discourages thinking through sketching; computers might also remove the designer from "the material." However, the computer can also liberate the designer from the repetitive nature of freehand drawing. Computer modeling also offers the designer, and others, virtual views of the imagined interior, and opportunities to combine computer drafting with freehand techniques to create hybrid drawings.

2 Robin Evans, *Translations from Drawing to Building and Other Essays*, London: AA Publications, 1997, p. 157

11. Concept stage

There are many methods of drawing that can be used to generate concepts and convey ideas about materials.

Thinking "through the material"

The materials that surround us can all be used as starting points to develop spatial concepts. The design process could begin with observational drawing, for example of a fir cone, shell, or a leaf. Drawings might be used to explore and examine the form, color, texture, and structure of the material world (materiality), and these drawings could be used to begin the design process.

Top two rows
Spatial and material concepts can begin by observing and recording the natural world.

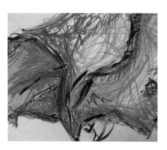  

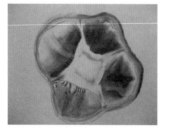  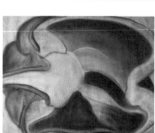

Bottom two rows
During and following a visit to the historic warship *HMS Warrior*, students completed observational and responsive drawings, took photographs, and created forms inspired by the ship. These observations were then the generators for studio-based experiments with materials and "drawings" made using threads, stitching, weaving, lacing, and knotting—processes that were ultimately translated into the spatial design propositions illustrated here.

 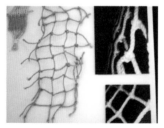 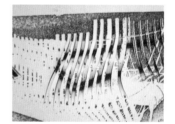

  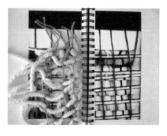

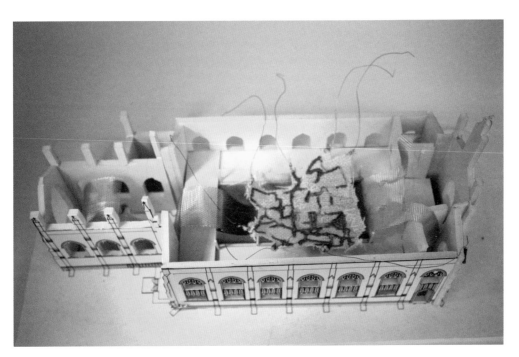

Left and below
A concept model and design proposal informed by the *HMS Warrior* project in the previous images, and a process-led approach to developing material concepts.

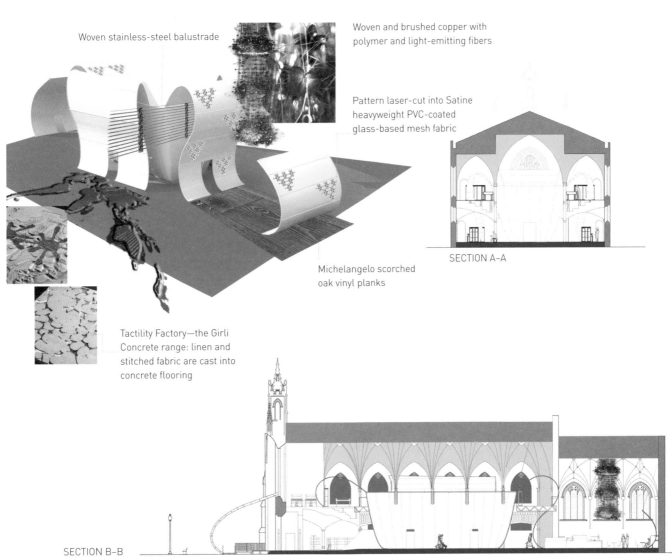

Woven stainless-steel balustrade

Woven and brushed copper with polymer and light-emitting fibers

Pattern laser-cut into Satine heavyweight PVC-coated glass-based mesh fabric

Michelangelo scorched oak vinyl planks

Tactility Factory—the Girli Concrete range: linen and stitched fabric are cast into concrete flooring

SECTION A–A

SECTION B–B

Below
Installation by Sarah Sze, *Just Now Dangled Still* at the Liverpool Biennial, 2008.

Below right
Jessica Stockholder's *Of Standing Float Roots in Thin Air*, 2006.

Artists Sarah Sze and Jessica Stockholder both use materials to investigate space, scale, color compositions, and juxtapositions of materials using found or discarded objects such as cotton bags, water bottles, oranges, clothes, and shipping containers. In response to the work and processes of these artists, design students at Portsmouth were able to "think through materials" by exploring the potential of found objects such as elastic, wool, chairs, stickers, and straws at the scale of a room; three-dimensional material sketches and generators for interior design concepts.

Thinking "through the sketch"

First thoughts are usually explored through sketches and models (three-dimensional sketches)—a process of playful thinking and experimentation coupled with analysis.

This sketching process could be a response to a thought or a concept (the designer has an idea and then sketches it), or the drawing and modeling process might generate thoughts (the designer models and sketches, and then has an idea about a spatial design). Sketching in this way is a non-linear and unpredictable process but may ultimately result in the "parti" sketch: a drawing or diagram that is a distillation of an overall concept for a design. Sketches can also be used as the design develops, to study and solve material interfaces and details (the micro).

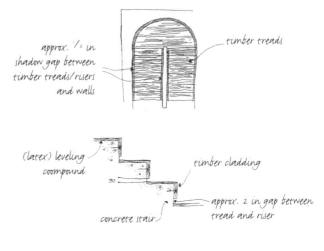

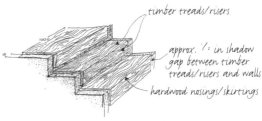

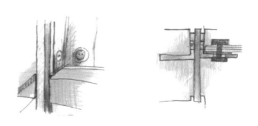

Right
As well as the overall idea (the macro) sketches are also used to solve material interfaces and details (the micro).

Left and below left
Michael Bates' drawings record his response to a site: the pace and rhythm of the space; movement and circulation; the objects within the space; aural experiences; and his personal, intellectual, and emotional response. Bates was particularly interested in movement: how the user of the space navigated boundaries, the user's physical interactions with the building, and the physical coming together and separation of people who inhabited the space. This drawn exploration of the site and the recording of his sensory experience led to the development of a spatial concept illustrated in the "parti" sketch and model, above. The sketch of the "big idea" (the macro) was then used to develop the overall form and associated materials.

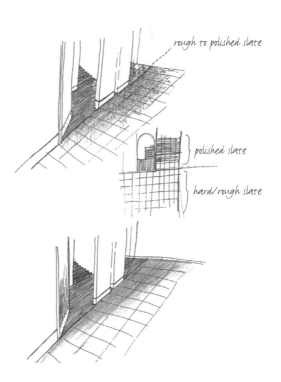

The sketchbook

Sketching is an essential and ongoing process of design, and the sketchbook an essential tool. The sketchbook can be used as a journal to observe and record ideas about materials; to question, evaluate, and reflect upon the recordings in a search for understanding and meaning; to plan areas to be developed and explore ideas, and to progress material concepts and designs.

Sketchbooks could contain some refined and detailed drawings, collages, paintings, and photographs. However, they are more likely to include many quick, analytical sketches or diagrams; drawing experiments; observational sketches of materials and associated sensory factors such as light, smells, textures, colors, and sounds; mind-maps; and measured site surveys and scribbled notes.

Although certainly used at the conceptual stage of the project, the sketchbook is an ongoing record of a creative and intellectual journey.

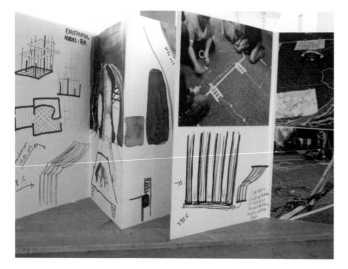

Left and below left
Images of students' sketchbooks, in which drawing was used to record and as a thinking tool.

Below
A collage that explores the optic–haptic experience of space. Abstract and conceptual representations of an interior can also be used to engage the audience and promote dialog. These methods encourage clarity of thought on the part of the designer: abstractions and distillations of ideas cannot be achieved unless there is a clear concept in place.

Freehand sketches and "drawings"

As ideas about materials begin to crystallize, designers will want to use a selection of methods to communicate their thinking in order to evoke the "spirit of place"; to communicate concepts; and to convey the sensory quality of a space and the atmospheres created using materials, material palettes, and juxtapositions of materials. These methods will vary according to intentions, and could be abstract/atmospheric drawings and paintings or more literal representations.

Sketch perspectives are one method, but the materials proposed for an interior space can also be described using techniques borrowed from the visual language of art: the use of abstraction and collage, assemblage and sculpture, printing, painting, and mark making. These artists' techniques use a broad range of materials, and can be used to describe the materials of an interior. Taking a creative and non-literal approach to drawing at this stage of a project can be an investigative and experimental process and can lead to unpredictable, significant outcomes.

When developing and representing ideas about material quality, it will be important to consider the effects of light within an interior. The designer will need to represent the quality of controlled natural light, which changes throughout the day, and also any artificial light used to enhance the interior experience. It is important that the designer develops techniques to convey this relationship between light and materials, with the light falling on different surfaces: textured, reflective, translucent, or opaque.

Below
Handrendering has been used here to communicate an interior atmosphere and representations of materials and light.

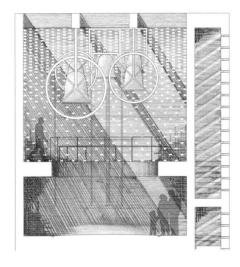

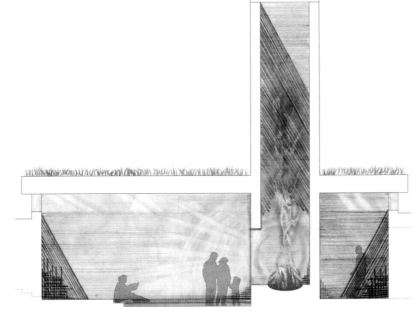

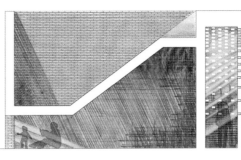

STEP BY STEP REPRESENTING MATERIAL ATMOSPHERES

Most designers develop their own style and methods of communicating material intentions through drawing. This exercise encourages an experimental approach to drawing, and to representing different materials and the atmospheres they create. Begin by identifying a poem that describes a particular material quality or atmosphere. Good reference poets include Sylvia Plath, Walt Whitman, T. S. Eliot, Samuel Taylor Coleridge, and Omar Khayyám. Write down some of the vocabulary from the poem that describes materials or atmosphere.

1 Collect and combine material samples that reflect the descriptions of materials and colors described in the poem (the material atmosphere). Assemble the materials to create a sculptural, spatial object.

2 Photograph the objects from different angles using natural and artificial lighting. Put a scaled figure into some of your photographs.

3 Choose your preferred object and light it from different angles. Prepare different media for your representational experiments.

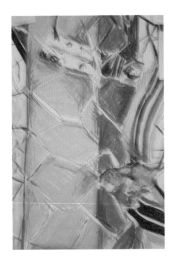
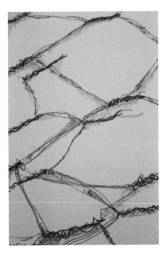

4 Draw one of the materials, or the assembly of materials, several times using tone only.

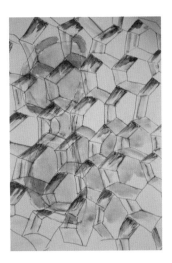

5 Repeat the exercise using different media and color.

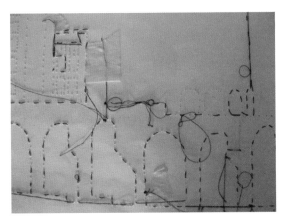

6 Try alternative methods of representing the materials, patterns, and textures. These examples use stitching, collage, and paint on fabric.

STEP BY STEP REPRESENTING EXISTING MATERIALS

Using stone as an example, this Step by Step presents different ways in which a material can be represented in order to express the atmosphere it can create. This may be done using a variety of media including photography, pencil drawing, color, painting, and photo manipulation.

1 Firstly select the material you wish to represent. In this Step by Step we are going to explore stone, but this method could be applied to any material.

2 The texture and surface of a material is emphasized when hit by light, so aim to complete this step on a bright day. Using tonal drawing (in this example, charcoal has been employed), record the quality of light in the space and the effects that this has on the material you are investigating.

3 Complete tonal drawings of material details using different media.

4 When light hits the surface of the stone, it does not merely affect brightness and contrast but it also illuminates the color of the material. In this case, the stone is very cool and gray but there are also hints of blues, mauve, and purple. Aim to record the subtle shifts in color that you observe.

5 Take photographs of the material using a macro lens so that you capture the fine details.

6 Using digital media, alter the image by changing the tonal contrast, color, or translucency.

7 With the help of digital media, use the photographs to represent the material in your own design. You could also try manipulating the scale of the material to see how this could transform your interior. Add images of people to give the image scale, and consider how the qualities of the material can be used to create different atmospheres.

Sketch models and conceptual models

Sketch models are very powerful tools at this stage of a project. Like drawings, the making process and experimental modeling can suggest solutions for projects; models can also be made to test alternative concepts and ideas about materials. It can be helpful to combine these methods with lighting and photography in order to explore the spatial potential suggested by the models.

The sketch model can be made to scale or as an abstract three-dimensional interpretation of an idea.

Scale models can have elements of the correct proportion within them, such as furniture, to help the viewer understand how activities may affect the space. A model can also have surfaces applied to it, in order to demonstrate how material applications affect the overall impression of the space.

Left and below
Experimental sketch models used to test alternative forms and color compositions: the models suggest a range of spatial design solutions.

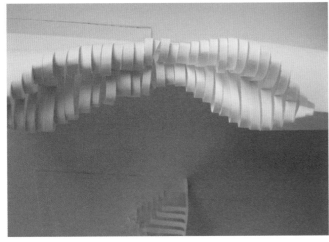

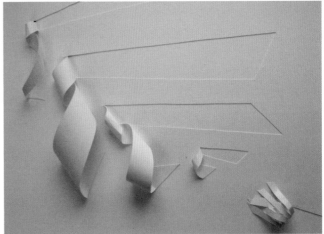

This page
The CAD interior design proposal shown at the top of the page was generated from a process of sketch modeling using paper, as shown in the models above.

Below left
Stacey Close created "linguistic collages" following a workshop with the novelist Tony White. In the workshop, White introduced experimental strategies (relating to narrative, morphology, grammar, and syntax) to explore new kinds of writing about place.

Below right
Words can be used to generate concepts, and can be combined with drawings to convey material atmospheres.

Materials vocabulary

Words can be used to generate concepts and to communicate ideas. This process could include the use of single words, a poem, or more extensive descriptive writing, which would elaborate on the atmospheric or phenomenological aspect of the materials—for example, how a materials feels, smells, or sounds. Words can be combined with drawings to clarify the intentions and to evoke impressions of a proposed interior.

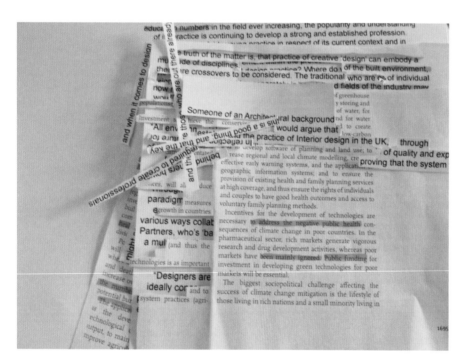

TIP BUILDING A VOCABULARY

It is important that designers develop an appropriate vocabulary of materials, which they can draw upon when developing concepts and when communicating verbally with other designers, clients, manufacturers, and contractors. This vocabulary may include scientific definitions, technical terminologies, the language of materials production and material finishes, and artistic or poetic descriptions.

Using digital media, list as many words as you can that are associated with materials. Order the words alphabetically and illustrate them with images or your own photographs.

As you encounter new words associated with materials, add them to your dictionary and include definitions where necessary.

Practice using appropriate vocabulary in your discussions and presentations about materials.

"Spirit of place" samples objects

Using physical materials to describe and discuss intentions is essential for the designer. As mentioned earlier in this book, many design studios are full of material samples that may be collected over long periods of time but that are also ordered for specific projects.

At the concept stage material solutions are not fixed, so samples might be presented as an assembly of "loose" products; however, other methods could also be used to convey intentions:

Collage or material models can be employed as techniques for composing and presenting materials. A sample board may comprise a series of layered textures, colors, and finishes that explores ideas about material relationships and proportions of color and tone.

Alternatively, materials might be assembled and combined in order to suggest ideas about the overall concept for a scheme—for example, the relationship between existing and new materials or ideas about lighting. With this approach, the challenge is to capture the essence of the design concept and express this idea through a sculptural object; this could be viewed as an equivalent of the "parti" sketch.

During the concept stage, it is essential for designers to explain their ideas and proposals using methods that are engaging and exciting, but that also promote critical thinking; this can make the difference between a project progressing or not, and will also inform the quality of the more developed design.

This page
Experimental models and material samples can be used to test ideas and communicate intentions.

Precedent images

When designing any type of space, it can be helpful to identify reference images or precedent projects that inspire conceptual thinking or help to communicate ideas to others—particularly the client.

It is important when responding to a project brief to investigate similar types of spaces. For example, if designing a restaurant, researching and analyzing other inspiring and successful restaurants can be helpful in resolving both functional and aesthetic issues, e.g. the relationship of the public and private areas, ideas for lighting, ceilings, and furniture. Alternatively, the precedent image may be selected not because the function is similar, but because it inspires in other ways—for example, the palette of materials that has been used.

The designer may also look to practitioners in other disciplines for inspiration. For example, how materials are used in different contexts, such as cloth in fashion, could be translated into a spatial design, or how materials are used in a particular piece of furniture could be adapted for an interior.

When sourcing images to communicate and represent ideas about materials, it must be clear why the reference is important: it could be the context of the material, the methods of assembly and construction, or a particularly unusual application of a material; it may be the texture, color, lighting, or juxtaposition of the material in a particular context. It is helpful to make some immediate notes in your sketchbook recording why you selected the image, as you may wish to refer back to it in the future.

It is good practice as a designer to build up folders or sketchbooks of ideas and references, both printed and digital. These can be used to record processes, design ideas, ways of drawing, and useful reference images and websites. The designer can build and refer to these sources when designing a particular project, but can also refer back to the folders to stimulate ideas for projects in the future. Note, all sources of information should be carefully referenced if used in presentations; referencing should include the name of the project, its date, and the name of the designer. If the image is intended to be published or reproduced in any way, then the photographer of the image should be contacted and permission agreed with them in advance.

This page

In this project, student Iwona Galazka has analyzed the work of Cinimod Studios (the precedent project was a frozen-yogurt shop, shown bottom row) and adapted Cinimod's inspirational use of light and color to suit her own concept (shown left).

12. Design development

Drawings and models

Once a design concept is agreed, drawings and models are used to develop a more robust and resolved design proposal. As described for the concept stage of a project, a wide range of methods can be used to test ideas and communicate the design intentions; however, these are likely to be different to those used earlier in the project.

CAD and freehand drawing techniques will still be used, but will be focused on articulating the proposals and spatial experience in more detail and to scale. A combination of drawings or composite drawings might be employed, including a range of two- and three-dimensional projections; for example, a combination of plans, rendered sections, elevations, axonometrics, and perspective drawings could be used.

At this stage, the perspective drawing is probably one of the most important methods that an interior designer can use to explore ideas and then present these ideas to a client. The perspective can be used to represent alternative views of the interior and can be used to describe the relationship of materials and light.

Physical models can also be used to great effect to communicate more detailed intentions, and are often a very seductive form of representation. They have value in themselves, but also as an object to photograph—the resulting images can be manipulated using the computer and presented as a set of alternative perspective views. Clients often respond well to models, as they can be easier to read than scale drawings.

Left and bottom left
Bird's-eye and straight-on views of a perspective model illustrating the material qualities, color, and patterns of a proposed interior.

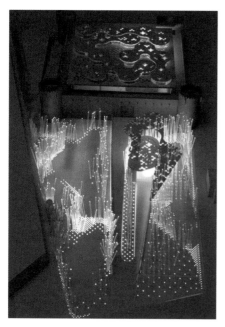

This page
Ushida Findlay Architects, Museum of National Textiles and Costumes, Qatar. Physical models were combined with CAD visualizations to test and communicate spatial concepts, inspired by the threading of fabric in Islamic art.

Computer-aided design (CAD) drawings

Computers can be used to create powerful and seductive images to suggest the qualities of imagined spaces. Computer images may be combined with freehand drawings and photographs of models to create evocative hybrid representations of an interior.

Many software packages allow materials and images to be scanned and combined with rendered drawings, and perhaps photographs, of the site; they can be used to create "photorealistic" impressions of space or more abstract interpretations.

CAD can also be used to explore the variables of an interior—such as alternative selections of colors, materials, and products—and how light may affect the surface of a material over the course of a day. The computer image can be amended quickly to show different combinations and juxtapositions of materials within the same space and with different qualities of light.

Below
A CAD visualization illustrating the interior qualities of lighting, pattern, wood, and reflective surfaces.

Bottom
Using InteriCAD 6000 3D rendering software, student Tony Tan tested alternative colors and materials in his winning design for the Janine Stone Young Interior Designer Award, 2011.

Above

To create this image, the following steps were taken by the Portsmouth University student Fiona Damiano:

1 A plan of the building was imported into SketchUp, and then was traced to create a three-dimensional model of the space.

2 A view was chosen (in this case, a view of the shop) and was rendered using Podium. This view was then saved as a JPEG.

3 The same view was then exported as a JPEG using different "styles" in SketchUp: one view being a "wireframe style," another "white with lines style," and finally a "colored transparent style."

4 These different JPEGs were then opened up in Photoshop, and all positioned in the same image as layers placed one on top of the other.

5 The "Podium rendered view" was placed on top of all these layers.

6 All the layers were then altered one by one by using the rubber in Photoshop: different areas on each layer were erased to reveal the layer beneath.

7 Some layers were further edited in Photoshop by desaturating them completely, by adding color and material, or by applying an artistic filter such as a sketchy style.

Sample boards and material products

One of the most useful tools that can be employed to communicate developed design proposals is the samples board or samples object (a sculptural assembly of materials). This can be presented alongside drawings and models in order to give a very complete representation of an interior.

As its name suggests, the samples board/object is a collection of the precise materials, colors, and finishes that are being proposed, and it can be coupled with larger samples of specific details and material products such as ironmongery or sanitary ware.

The sample board/object can take many forms and is, in itself, a design exercise. Its materials need to be combined and composed in correct proportions, and also as an expression of the design concept. If the scheme has a minimalist concept, then this should be reflected in the way material samples are organized and assembled; if bright orange is used as an accent color in the scheme, then the paint swatch on the samples board should be represented at the same proportion to other materials and not dominate the board.

Traditionally, sample boards are arranged on panels of wood or cardboard. If this is the approach used, materials may be window mounted (framed by the board) or a combination of surface mounted and inset: the board is likely to have depth in order to accommodate the various thicknesses of materials. However, the presentation of such samples could be three-dimensional and "sculptural," and perhaps a specially designed case, box, set of drawers, or hinged "cupboards" could be designed and made as an extension of the concept and for practical purposes. The solution should be creative and demonstrate your design integrity and conceptual thinking. The designer should also consider how the materials are to be transported and exhibited, as it is possible that they will be presented at several different meetings in different locations.

In addition to this traditional technique, digital sample boards could be generated for a computer-based presentation. Images of samples can be used from the Internet (these must be carefully referenced and sourced), and materials can be scanned and composed. This approach has its uses; however, it removes the viewer from the tactile nature of real materials and surfaces, textures, smells, etc. such that these cannot be fully appreciated and understood.

The sample board and material products are often used to agree and "sign off" the design before the detailed drawing, specification, and documentation process is commenced.

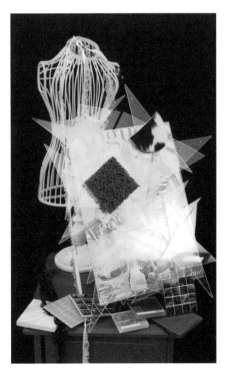

Left
Presentation samples need not be simply arranged flat on panels. These examples show more innovative ways to display samples.

STEP BY STEP PRESENTING MATERIAL SAMPLES

Materials are often presented to clients and other interested parties at different stages of a project to communicate and discuss initial thoughts, to show developed ideas, or present prototypes.

The exercise illustrated here encourages the designer to think about how samples are assembled in order to communicate preferred material intentions, and how the choice of materials relates to the overall design concept.

1 Consider the relationship between the materials you have selected and the overall design concept. How do the materials express and reinforce this concept? How do they relate to those of the existing context?

2 Gather your material samples and consider how they can be assembled to reflect the overall concept of your scheme. Will the materials be presented on a board? Window mounted or framed? Presented as a sculptural or spatial object? Does the form or composition relate to the site, design concept, sectional drawings, or plans?

3 Consider the proportions of the materials you are composing. Do they reflect the proportions that will be used in your interior design? Test the relationship of material finishes and colors. Are there alternatives that might be more successful?

4 Once you have decided upon the appropriate proportion of materials to be used and the approximate format, begin testing alternative arrangements.

5 When you have finalized your composition, assemble your materials using precise methods of cutting, fixing, and fastening. You could use this opportunity to express the relationship between the overall concept and the material details (the macro and the micro scales).

13. Detail and construction stage

Detail and working drawings

Detail drawings are used to resolve functional and aesthetic relationships between materials and to communicate the finalized design. These drawings can convey information that will permit the interior to be "costed" (how much it will cost to build), and allow contractors to understand the designer's intention and construct the interior; they can also be used to agree construction methods with specialist contractors/consultants.

Left and opposite
A student has combined a tenth-of-full-size detail drawing (opposite) with a visualization (left) to communicate how her design will be constructed and the intended appearance. The red square on the left highlights the area shown in detail opposite.

SECTION DETAIL SCALE 1½":1'0"
1. 3½ x ½ x ¹⁄₁₆ in Karndean—Michelangelo
     scorched oak vinyl planks
     screed
     underfloor heating
     thermal insulation
     DPM
     concrete slab
2–4. recycled aluminum
5. stainless-steel bracket bolted to tensile frame
6. steel angle
7. EPPM intermediate layer
8. gray imitation suede polyester fabric
9. polyurethane upholstery
10. 1 in molded fiberboard element
11. ⅛ in translucent acrylic glass
12. fluorescent tube
13. fiberboard
14–15. timber section
16 heavyweight PVC-coated glass-based mesh fabric
17 ⅛ in stainless-steel cable attached to open swage socket
18 steel frame
19 woven fiber mesh sandwiched between toughened
     safety glass with a beveled edge

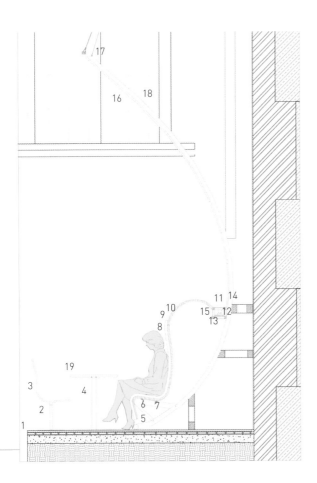

At this stage of a project, different scales of drawing are necessary to explain the design intentions: how materials are juxtaposed; joints, junctions, fixings, fastenings; the relationship between different types of materials (structural, decorative, acoustic, hygienic, etc.). The drawings will also be used to locate various aspects of the interior and coordinate building services, such as ducts and light fittings, with ceilings and partitions. These drawings can be referred to as "working drawings," they inform the process of building and making a space or an element within a space, and they will be "worked to" by the building contractor, manufacturer, or installer. Sometimes these are developed in conjunction with, or by, the contractor. (For more on detail and construction drawings see case studies on pages 178 and 180.)

Detail drawings can be at 1'0":1'0" (full size). This scale allows a very close inspection of materials, how they fit together and integrate with other elements of the interior. There may be a particularly difficult condition in a space, which needs careful thought; 1:1 scale allows this level of interrogation, and can explain how something very complex needs to be assembled or built.

Other scales, for example 6":1'0", 3":1'0", and 1½":1'0" allow different kinds of exploration and explanation. If a drawing is one-tenth real scale, then it is clear that it is not suitable for the communication of surface details, but the position of elements adjacent to one another—for example, on a door or a piece of designed furniture or fitting—can be communicated. 6":1'0" and 3":1'0" scales are often used to describe the detail of joints, junctions, and assembly. The ¾":1'0" scale will often be used to indicate the location of details (drawn at 6":1'0" scale, etc.). Other scale drawings will also be developed by interior designers, architects, and engineers to coordinate, for example, building services and to set out (position) lighting.

All of the above drawings will then be contextualized in ¼":1'0", ⅛":1'0", and possibly ¹⁄₁₆":1'0" drawings, to form a coherent set of documents that describes the interior in full. The completed set—along with the specification, described overleaf—forms the construction package that is sent to the building contractor(s).

DRAWING CONVENTIONS

When preparing technical drawings that describe material details, the designer will often employ recognized drawing conventions. The diagrams below provide some examples; drawing conventions are also described in reference books and industry guidelines.

Stonework

Brickwork

Blockwork

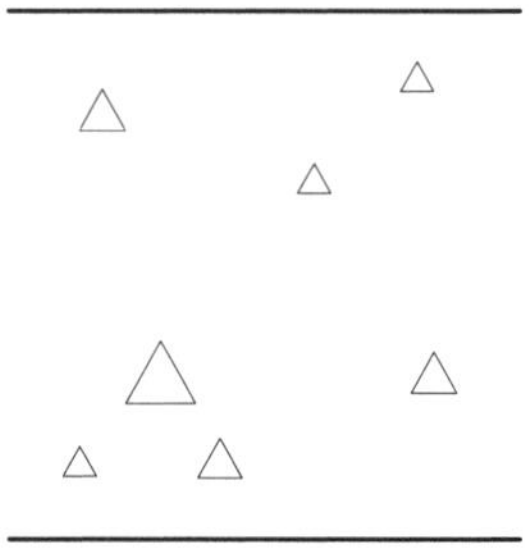

Concrete

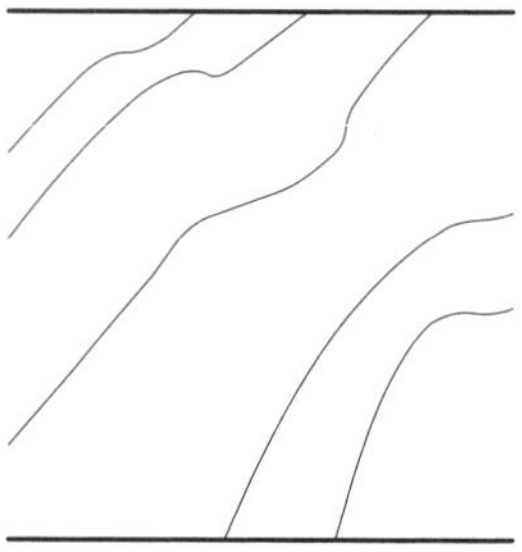

Softwood

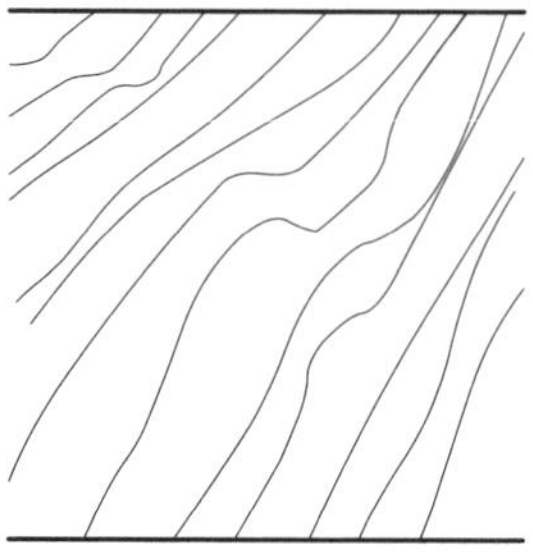

Hardwood

Plasterboard

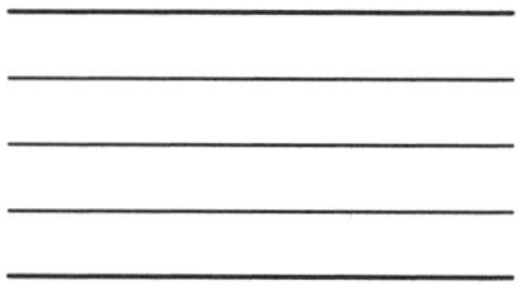

Plywood

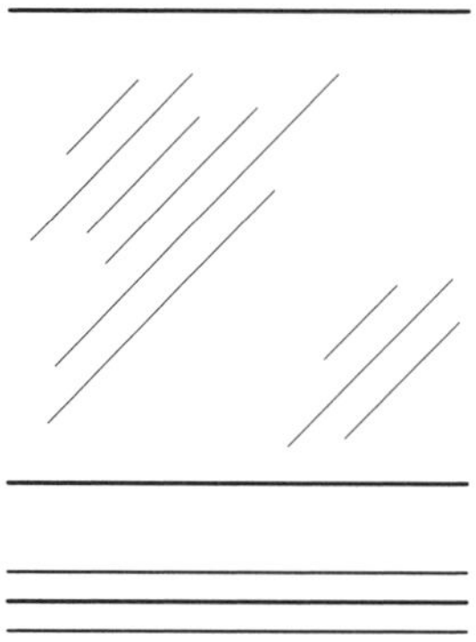

Glazing

Written representation and description

Once the client has agreed to the materials selected and approved the cost, the designer can then specify the product.

At this stage, interiors are described through a language of specification, for example: cavity wall, leveling compound, suspended ceiling, stud partition, fair-faced brick, tiled flooring, adhesive, book-match veneer, lacquered finish, and plaster finish. Specification is the process by which the designer confirms to the client, the design team, and the building contractor the precise material or product that has been agreed and how it is to be built; the material can then be purchased and assembled as part of the construction package. A specification is often read in conjunction with a set of drawings that locate the material and describe the construction details.

Materials can also be identified in a Bill of Quantities. This document itemizes all the materials to be used in a space, like a list of ingredients, so they can be measured, quantified, and costed by the designer or a quantity surveyor. For example, the area of timber specified by the designer can be measured and quantified, allowing the price for the purchase and installation of this material to be estimated. This is a very useful way to understand how much the overall project will cost, and also allows an understanding of how the selection of alternative materials can reduce or increase cost.

Below and overleaf
In practice, material specifications can be communicated in words only but also often appear with visual references in the form of specification sheets, as illustrated below and on the following pages. This form of documentation provides a clear and helpful reference for the designer, the client, and the contractor. Based on data sheets generated by Freehand Projects, the specification sheets illustrated here describe the product name and color, the supplier or manufacturer's details, and can also be used to communicate associated costs.

Fabrics

Ref: FN006 Location: Focus

Rooms
Item: Furniture Upholstery
Trade name: DIVINA2
Manufacturer: KVADRAT
Specification:
- 100% new wool fabric
- 45.000 Martindale Rub Test index
- Use double stitching on all upholstery seams in thread color to match fabric
- Ref. 224 WARM GREY for acoustic ceiling panel in Focus Room
- Ref. 334 TAUPE for Reception/Partner Sofa
- Ref. 552 TERRACOTTA for Reception/Touchdown Armchairs
- Ref. 671 AUBERGINE for Operational Chairs

Ceiling Finishes

Ref: FN008 Location: EA/CSSA

Item: Acoustic Ceiling Tile
Trade name: Offecct, Soundwave®Flo
Specification:
• White acoustic tile/24 x 24 mm, applied to plasterboard ceiling for improved acoustics
• Recyclable molded polyester fiber upholstered in white wool fabric

Armchair and Footrest

Ref. FU002 Location: Reception

Item: Armchairs
Trade name: EGG
(the original Fritz Hansen Egg™ Chair, designed by Arne Jacobsen)
Manufacturer: FRITZ HANSEN
Specification:
• Fabric DIVINA2 KVADRAT

Prototypes

Prototypes are full-size representations of part of an interior that can be built by the main building contractor or specialist subcontractors, either on site or in their workshop. The prototype can be used to test a particularly unusual configuration or use, or the performance of a material, prior to constructing the interior; alternative methods and materials may be used, and the prototype can be assessed by all relevant members of the design team and approved by the client.

Post-construction and occupation

Once the interior has been constructed, there are some final forms of representation and communication that will need to be completed. These include:

Punch lists: this is a list of concerns about the finished interior that can be identified by the client or designer; it relates specifically to the build quality and whether the building corresponds with the construction drawings and specifications. The list of items is then handed to the contractor to address.

A set of "as built" drawings: this is a set of drawings that describe in full what has been built. These are useful documents for the client and can be referred to in future if further works are completed or if there are specific areas of the interior that require access or maintenance but are not easily accessed.

The Operations and Maintenance Manual: this document is handed to the client when the project is complete, and it is particularly important for larger projects. It includes information about how interior elements are operated and serviced; for example, if a material has been specified that requires specialist cleaning and maintenance this will be identified in the manual and the cleaning methods described. The manual will also include information about the mechanical and electrical installations such as lighting and power, security installations, and mechanical ventilation systems, and will identify the suppliers of, for example, new lamps for the light fittings or of audiovisual equipment.

Finally, when the building is complete it is often represented photographically. Photographs are used by clients to promote their new building, and designers add these photographs to their portfolio; the images can also be used in books and design journals. This photographic record can be inspirational to other designers and clients, it may form part of design archives and can ultimately inform historical accounts of the interior, as illustrated earlier in this book. One might question the following claim by Swiss architects Herzog and de Meuron, but the statement is thought-provoking:

And afterward, once the project has been finalized and the building completed, the representation of the work in photographs has become just as important, if not more important than, the building itself.[3]

3 Jacques Herzog and Pierre de Meuron, *Herzog & de Meuron, Natural History*, Canadian Centre for Architecture and Lars Muller Publishers, 2002, p. 399.

PART V MATERIAL CLASSIFICATIONS, PROCESSES, AND SOURCES

Many designers work with a palette of "favorite" materials that they have tested, collected, and stored over several years; however, good designers are also likely to be alert to shifting trends and material innovations and will search for supplements or alternatives to the familiar palette.

This section will include some of the material sources and resources available to the designer searching for information and material products. It also introduces material types, processes, and methodologies for classifying, describing, and organizing materials.

Left

Materia Inspiration Center, Amsterdam. Associated with the online resource Materia (see page 157), this physical showroom has an inspirational collection of new materials and provides opportunities for practitioners from different disciplines to share knowledge and ideas. There are other similar resources across the globe.

14. Material classifications

The way designers classify and organize materials, both physically (such as in a library) or when searching for products, will inform their practice and the interiors they create. It is good for a designer to challenge preconceptions about materials, such as the way they are indentified, understood (in terms of appropriate applications), named, and grouped, and to consider alternative ways of knowing "all about" a material.

Materials can be classified and archived according to their mechanical properties, which the designer will assess when considering the intended function of the material, for example:

Strength materials can be classed as strong or weak according to their ability to resist stress;

Stiffness materials can be stiff or flexible according to their ratio of applied stress to elastic strain;

Plasticity if a material has plasticity in tension it is described as being ductile; if it has plasticity in compression then it is described as being malleable;

Toughness a material can be tough or brittle—this relates to how much energy a material absorbs before it fractures;

Hardness a material can be classed as hard or soft according to its ability to resist surface indentation.

Materials might also be classified according to their likely function or intended application; for example, materials that are used for ceilings could be grouped together as could materials that are used as floor finishes, partitions, etc. Although this is a logical archiving system to use in practice and serves its purpose well in some situations, it can prevent more creative, exciting possibilities, such as using a material outside its original intended context (its reappropriation).

The designer might also adopt a method of classification and organization that corresponds approximately with scientific definitions of materials. Using this conventional, "scientific" method recognizes that a single material could fulfill multiple functions: wood could be used as a floor finish, but it might also be specified as a wall or ceiling panel; it might be specified because of its structural integrity, or as a decorative surface; it could be considered a warm, durable hardwearing floor material or a surface that requires considerable care. However, this method of classification can still be predictable and can be challenged by some contemporary materials that do not fit these definitions—for example, composite materials, which are made from two or more substances, or "smart" materials that are designed to respond to the environment, such as shape-memory alloys or piezoelectric ceramics.

Testing alternative methods of classifying materials can encourage the designer to think laterally and explore the potential of materials, as the images overleaf illustrate.

On the following pages we have used the broadly scientific classifications of materials to provide descriptions of the different materials available for interior design, and the associated material finishes and processes.

Classification 1 Grouped according to common names. This is a familiar method of storing materials in a practice. However, groupings are inconsistent, in some places referring to the form that the material takes (film or carpet) or in others, to the scientific classification of material (glass).

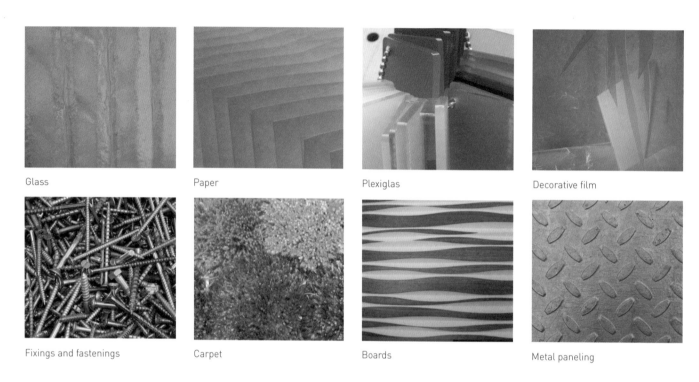

Glass

Paper

Plexiglas

Decorative film

Fixings and fastenings

Carpet

Boards

Metal paneling

Classification 2 Corresponds, broadly, with scientific classifications of materials.

Ceramic (including glass)

Glass

Metal

Polymers

Wood

Natural fibers

Composites

Stone

Classification 3 Grouped according to
the material's likely application.

Flooring

Upholstery

Decorative film

Surface decoration

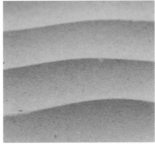

Surface decoration

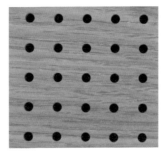

Acoustic paneling

Classification 4 Grouped according to
the material's sensory properties.

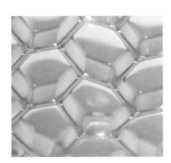

Transparent / translucent

Transparent / translucent

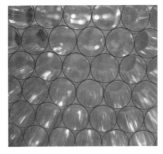

Transparent / translucent

Soft

Soft

Soft

Below
Woven plastic.

Below right
In Lauren Moriarty's Noodle Block Light, heat-formed rubber has been laser cut to create a "3D textile" cube.

Polymers

Polymers encompass naturally occurring materials such as rubber, shellac, and cellulose, and also include synthetic or semisynthetic materials—for example, Bakelite, polypropylene, nylon, and silicone (all have been widely used in interior design).

Polymers can be manipulated using thermosetting and thermoplastic processes—these processes make the material temporarily more malleable and/or ductile. Some polymers heated using these methods can be easily molded using techniques such as casting, injection molding, and rotational molding; as the materials cool they set hard in their new form. Polymers can also be cut using water jets and laser cutting, and "laminated" using stereolithography. These processing methods are used to create a vast range of mass-produced and one-off products: chairs, tables, cladding, etc.

The strength, toughness, and ductility of plastics vary greatly, so suitability for the intended function needs to be checked carefully. Designers must also be aware that some plastics are known to be toxic to the environment, although increasingly they are being developed using 100 percent biodegradable and organic materials such as starch and cellulose.

There are dozens of polymeric materials that can be used in interiors, such as plastic laminates, plastic cladding, plastic sheet materials, and rubber flooring. Different finishes can be applied to these materials during the manufacturing process, such as textures, indented or relief patterns, or laminated finishes; once the polymer has taken its form, the materials can then also be screen-printed, cut, polished, and coated with decorative or protective finishes.

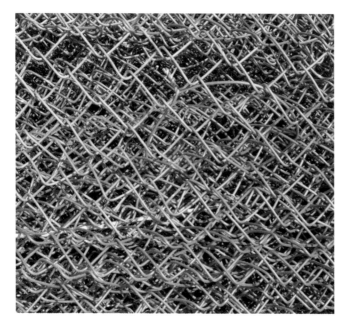

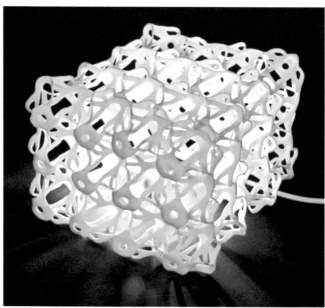

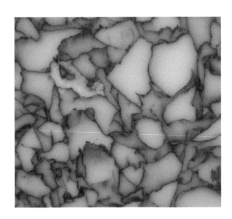

Top row
Polymers can be manufactured in many colors, surface textures, and levels of translucency.

Left
Mandarina Duck flagship store, Paris, 2001, by NL Architects with Droog Design. A wall of elastic bands is used to display merchandise.

Below left and right
Anna Siedlecka and Radek Achramowicz of Puff-Buff Design designed the low-voltage-light "Superstar" chandelier using inflated, high-frequency welded, PVC film (phthalate free). Each "bubble" has its own valve and a single LED light point.

Metals

Metals account for 75 percent of the elements in the Periodic Table—for example, tin, lead, aluminum, zinc, titanium, mercury, iron, copper, and cobalt. Metal elements can be combined with other metallic or nonmetallic materials, such as carbon, to create alloys—for example, iron is combined with carbon to create steel, which is harder and has a greater tensile strength than pure iron.

Metals tend to be strong and ductile, although their mechanical properties also vary greatly: some metals, such as nickel alloys, resist corrosion; titanium can be stronger at high temperatures than other metals; aluminum is easy to form; and iron and steel are used in construction for their strength.

Metals can be formed using various processes, such as casting and molding, laser cutting, panel beating, tube bending, metal spinning, and metal stamping. Metals are very often used for structure and as a cladding material, but also in product design such as ironmongery and for fixings and fastenings: nails, rivets, hinges, clamps, etc. Designers select metals for interior projects for their functionality, but also based on their aesthetic qualities, which will vary according to the metal's inherent properties, e.g. the color of copper or bronze. However, the aesthetic qualities of metals can also be transformed by the finishes applied to them: metals can be pressed or indented with a surface texture and patterns can be applied using screen-printing, perforation, bead blasting, or photo-resist acid etching. They can be abraded, hammered, burnished, oxidized, anodized, oiled, or polished, and coatings can be applied using electroplating or powder-coating. These all present numerous possibilities for the designer to explore.

This page
Metals produced in various forms including mesh, perforated sheet metal, ridged copper, and corrugated aluminum.

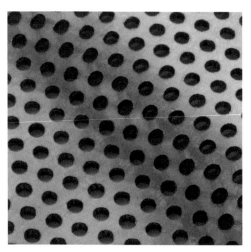

Below
In their design for Mandarina Duck's flagship store in Paris, NL Architects and Droog Design also designed an "inverse clothes rack." Inspired by the forms of clothes on hangers, they created a cocoon with seamless joints from brushed aluminum.

Right
Zaha Hadid Architects created a metallic, deconstructivist intervention at a point of transition within Monsoon restaurant in Sapporo, Japan.

Wood and other organic fibers

Woods and other natural materials such as bamboo, cork, cotton, wool, silk, and hemp are organic, fibrous, composite materials. They have various qualities, including strength and stiffness, and can be recycled and renewed if sources are correctly managed; they also have sensory qualities that can be appealing, such as inherent natural odors, textures, and colors.

Wood can be processed to create veneers, composite block, and board materials, and may also be formed using lathes, saws, laser cutting, separating methods, wood turning, and steam bending.

Like metal, different woods have different functional and aesthetic characteristics, and finishes can be applied to transform appearance and protect the material. Wood can be waxed or sealed using shellac, varnish, or oil (these processes can impregnate the wood with the scent of lemons, linseed, or beeswax). They may be sanded, scraped and polished using wire wool, pumice, and fabric pads; stains and paint can be applied in order to color and protect the material; lacquering can also be applied, to provide heat resistance and to create a high gloss, satin, or matte finish.

Below
Design Spirits' design for the Niseko Look Out Cafe, Hokkaido, Japan. A vertical timber lattice, known to represent Japanese identity, is used to create seating booths, walls, and ceiling.

Below right
Various samples of wood/timber-based products including Art Wood, bamboo (from the Bamboo Flooring Company), milled MDF, and Flakeboard (laminated timber flakes).

Art Wood

Milled MDF

Mahogany

Beech

Flakeboard

Bamboo

Paper, a product of wood and other organic materials, is also used in interiors for a range of functions—for example, wallpaper, wall panels, and screens such as the *shoji* screens used in Japan. Paper or paper pulp is a versatile material and can be processed using many techniques, such as pressing, molding, and casting, to create a range of translucent and opaque forms. Similarly, cardboard can be used to create lightweight but strong forms.

Organic yarns—such as wool, silk and cotton—are used extensively in interior design, for curtains, upholstery, screens, carpets, rugs, light fittings, and acoustically absorbent or decorative cladding. Processing methods include pressing, molding, weaving, tufting, and knotting—the resulting fabrics can be stitched, fastened, or glued to create a range of forms and surfaces.

Below left
Product designers MIO use compressed, molded paper to create wall and ceiling tiles.

Below right
Woodstock, a decorative wallpaper manufactured by Cole and Son.

Bottom left
"Papercut," designed for the Yeshop fashion showroom in Athens, Greece, by dARCHstudio (Elina Drossou with collaborators Nikos Karkatselas, Chrysa Konstantinidou, and 10 volunteers). The project incorporates 100% recyclable materials including thousands of sheets of corrugated cardboard packaging and low-cost OSB (oriented strand board). The biomorphic construction was inspired by the human body.

Right
Anne Kyyro Quinn makes interior textiles using hand-cut, sewn, and finished natural fabrics such as felt.

Center right
A woven-fabric rug.

Bottom right
Silk.

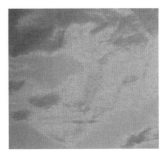

Ceramics and glass

Ceramic is a wonderful material; malleable and pliable, it can be pushed and pulled, squeezed, molded, poured, and ground.[1]

Ceramics are nonmetallic materials that can be slip-cast, thrown, molded, or formed and fired at high temperatures to create various products such as floor and wall tiles, mosaics, crockery, and sanitary ware. Ceramic products are generally resistant to moisture and high temperatures; they can be strong, hard, wear-resistant, and tend to be brittle. Ceramics can be textured or smooth, slip- and frost-resistant, they can be pigmented or painted, and glazes can be applied during the firing process. Bricks, an ancient product primarily made from clay, are "ceramic" and can be used for their structural integrity, warm colors, and decorative potential. Bricks are modular components (8 x 3⅝ x 2¼ in is the standard US size) and can be laid in rows (known as courses) and in different arrangements (known as bonds, for example Flemish Bond, Stretcher Bond, etc.).

Glass (also considered part of the ceramics "family") has been used for millennia for products, jewelry, decoration, and glazing. More recently, methods of blowing and processing glass have produced a widened array of products and uses: structural glazing, thermal insulators, glass-fiber-reinforced concrete, and glass-fiber-reinforced plastics; glass is also essential to fiberoptics and telecommunications technologies.

Glass can be tempered or laminated for security purposes; fabrics, metal meshes, and other materials can be "captured" between laminated layers to creative decorative finishes. "Smart" glass can literally be switched so that the transmission of light is altered (from transparent to opaque) when electricity passes through the material.

A number of finishes can be achieved during the glass-manufacturing process: metals can be added to the material or applied to the surface in order to create iridescent or dichroic effects. Glass can be acid etched or sandblasted to create patterns and to achieve different degrees of translucency; CVC machining can be used to cut glass; and colored pigments can be added or color applied using screen-printing or back painting.

1 Chris Lefteri, *Materials for Inspirational Design*, Brighton: RotoVision, 2006, p. 6.

Below
"Pict," a modular partitioning product designed by Fred & Fred, uses frosted glass blocks with numerous integral optical lenses that refract light. This design provides luminosity without the need for electricity.

Below center
The installation "Indigo" was designed by Jurgen Bey for Droog Design for Levi's Red Line. Using liquid crystal technologies, the laminated glass constantly shifts its appearance from transparent to translucent indigo. As electrical charges transform the glass, the clothing displayed is revealed and then appears to sink back into a pool of indigo.

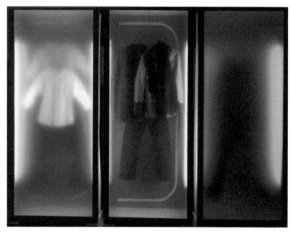

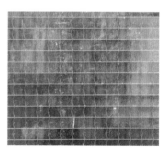

Left
Examples of wired and cast glass.

Stone and slate

Naturally occurring materials such as stone (including granite, marble, and limestone) and slate are extracted from the earth, processed, and used in the built environment.

Stone can be used in the form of modular blocks, slabs, paviours, and tiles of very different sizes (from ½ in square stone mosaics to slabs that can be more than 39 in in length). Stone can also be chiseled and cut into complex forms.

Stone floor tiles are usually ¾–1⅛ in thick and can be laid on a sand bed or bonded to a level substrate. Stone laminates are also now available—thinner stone tiles are bonded to rigid sheet polymers, metal, or particle boards.

The functional properties of stone can vary greatly. Granite, for example, is a very hard material and is nonporous; it is often used as a floor finish, as a cladding material, or for kitchen and bathroom worktops. Other stones such as marble, limestone, and slate can be used in these contexts but they are softer and less moisture-resistant, so the application and finishing needs to be considered carefully. Travertine is pitted and would be inappropriate for an interior environment that is dusty or polluted (where cooking fats are used, for example) unless the holes were filled.

These materials are available in numerous colors (with natural variations) and finishes: polished, hewn, rough-hewn, honed, and hammered. Stone chips can also be combined with cement or resin-based materials to create composites such as Terrazzo.

Stone is a durable, high-quality, expensive material but it is derived from finite sources that are not renewable.

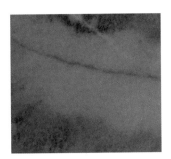

Marble

This page
A selection of stone types and forms including marble, sandstone, and limestone, and setts, blocks, and cobbles. The images illustrate some of the range of colors, patterns, textures, finishes, and modules available.

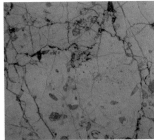

Marble

Marble

Portland limestone blocks

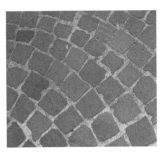

Granite setts

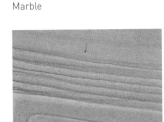

Sandstone

Jura limestone

Cobble paving

Irregular granite paving

Animal products

Animal "products" such as ivory, leather/skin, fur, shell, and bone have also been used in interior design (consider the materials of the Art Deco period). Leather is still used widely for upholstery, but also as a cladding and flooring material, while mother-of-pearl is used to create decorative tiles. Trading in many other such products is now illegal, as the species involved are protected—for example, elephants in the case of ivory. However, these materials are still valued and purchased by some people. Synthetic alternatives to all animal-derived products are available.

Animal fur

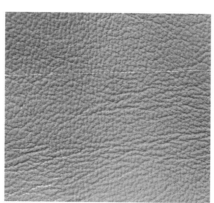

Synthetic leather

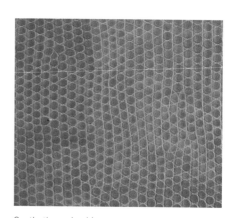

Synthetic snakeskin

Mother-of-pearl tile

Leather flooring

Composites

Many of the materials discussed in these pages can also be defined as composites, a combination of more than one material element. Steel is a composite; other familiar examples include epoxy resins, fiberglass, and concrete.

Concrete is an ancient building material that does not fit any of the above "scientific classifications." Owing to its potential strength and versatility, it is used in contemporary buildings more than any other man-made material. Concrete is made from cement; a substance such as lime, which sets hard and can bind other materials; coarse aggregates, such as crushed stone; fine aggregates, such as sand; and finally water (although other chemicals can be added depending upon the application). The "recipe" chosen for the concrete mix will affect its appearance and physical properties. For example, concrete can be "foamed" (air bubbles are entrained within the mix) to create a lighter, more frost-resistant product or glass-fiber optical strands can be added to create a light transmitting product (see page 27).

Like other materials that are poured or cast, concrete can have different surface textures. This can be achieved by selecting shuttering or formwork (used to contain the concrete before it sets hard) with a particular pattern such as wood grain. Surface texture will also vary according to the size of the aggregate. Concrete can also be supplied in precast units that can be assembled quickly on site.

There are environmental concerns associated with the sourcing of materials, manufacturing processes, and disposal; however, efforts are being made by the concrete industry to improve sustainability; for example, waste paper pulp is now being used as a form of cement.

Stucco (or plaster) is a similar, cementitious material that is also used extensively in interior environments. Plaster can be colored, mixed with fine aggregates or glass, and can be applied using different techniques to create a range of finishes. Historically, plaster was also used as a surface upon which to paint and decorate— examples have been found in Roman villas. Today, plasterboard (rigid panels made from plaster) is a ubiquitous material that can be used to construct walls and can be finished using plaster skim coats (smooth or textured), paper, decorative paneling, and paint.

Contemporary materials are often categorized as composites: for example, biopolymers that use biodegradable materials derived from rice husks, soya, maize, and corn; "plastic woods" that combine polymers with recycled wood flour; laser-sintered materials; elastic synthetic materials; Dupont Corian® and other similar solid surfacing materials, which combine acrylic and aluminum trihydrate; and numerous other products that combine recycled metals, stones, plastics, and ceramic materials.

These and many other traditional materials can be processed using contemporary, computer-aided technologies to design and make elaborate forms.

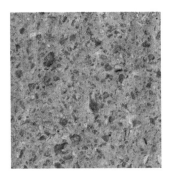

Top left
Concrete can be cast to achieve many different surface textures.

Above
Concrete can be mixed with various sizes of aggregate to get different colors and textures.

Left
Concrete steps at the Castelvecchio Museum.

Above, above left, and left
Original painted plaster walls at the Castelvecchio Museum.

New and emerging materials and processes

In Part 1 of this book we referred to the transformative effect nascent digital technologies are having on spatial design. However, as these new methods are at an early stage of their evolution, it is difficult to predict how they will continue to shape the creation, manufacture, and application of materials. Research and product prototyping by designers and scientists, often in collaboration, suggest many tantalizing possibilities.

Materials development

Materials that have been developed and are continuing to emerge from academic research and scientific and industrial endeavor have characteristics that were unimaginable in previous generations. A few examples are outlined below but there are many more alternatives.

Nanotechnology is one of the most significant areas of research in materials science and refers to the development and manipulation of synthetic materials at the atomic or molecular level.

Graphene is a material that is only one atom thick and believed to be the strongest material ever measured: "Graphene does not just have one application," says Professor Andre Geim, the current co-holder of the Nobel Prize in physics for his work with the material at Manchester University. "It is not even one material. It is a huge range of materials. A good comparison would be to how plastics are used."[2]

Nanotechnology-enabled materials and processes result in products that are smaller, lighter, stronger, and cheaper than traditional alternatives. For example, carbon nanotubes (CNTs) are super-strong, resilient materials and could be used in the future to replace steel and concrete to create lightweight structures. Nanotubes could be used to create "gossamer structures that open up spatial realms far beyond anything we could imagine ... nanoscale structures would be like clouds."[3] Nanotechnology is also beginning to inform the development of smart materials used in the interior.

Smart materials are composite materials that are capable of reacting to external stimuli; the reactions can be defined as sensory, adaptive, or active. For example, sensory materials could have built-in sensors that detect changes in the material's structure; adaptive materials might change their color or volume in response to environmental conditions such as heat and light; and active materials have both sensors and actuators and are capable of complex behavior—they can sense changing conditions and adapt to them.[4] These "living" materials have various applications in the interior and include materials that can absorb smells, detect and absorb bioagents, and change color if they are about to break or in response to heat and light (thermochromic or photochromic). Such materials might possess shape memory, or the ability to collect light during the day and release it after dark. Some can even self-extinguish in the case of fire and clean and repair themselves.

Materials processing

Digital processes coupled with more traditional methods of manipulating materials have created new opportunities for the innovative designer. As well as digitally processing new materials, digital technologies can also be used to "reimagine" and configure familiar materials such as brick.

Contemporary processes include:

Two-dimensional processes: digitally controlled water jet cutting and laser cutting.

Subtractive processes: computer numerical control (CNC) milling.

Additive processes: three-dimensional printing, rapid prototyping, stereolithography, laser sintering, and laminated object manufacturing.

Robotics: used to translate and connect digitally designed space with the material reality.

The examples illustrated on these pages and similar research projects suggest that robotics will be used not only in the manufacturing of materials but also in building construction, where materials will be assembled and connected with efficiency and precision. It is also clear that materials science will transform our understanding of materiality and material realities.

It is important that the designer remains informed about new and emerging materials and processes and understands how to find and store information.

2 http://news.bbc.co.uk/1/hi/programmes/ click_online/9491789.stm (03.10.11).
3 Erik Baard, "Unbreakable" in *Architecture*, June 2001, p. 52.
4 Branko Kolarevic, *Architecture in the Digital Age: Design and Manufacturing*, London: Taylor & Francis, 2003, p. 51.

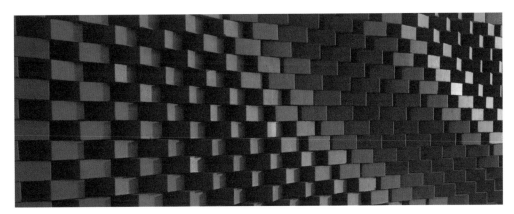

Left

The Programmed Wall, ©Gramazio & Kohler, ETH Zürich. Using digital fabrication methods and robotics, the design potential of traditional brick was challenged. In accordance with algorithmic programs, a robot laid 400 bricks, each in a slightly different location and rotation in space.

Left

Procedural Landscapes 2, ©Gramazio & Kohler, ETH Zürich. Decorative concrete panels are usually created using subtractive processes, which can be efficient for large-scale production of identical units, but are wasteful on a smaller scale. As a more efficient alternative, students at ETH Zürich used digital robotic fabrication methods and granular materials such as sand to create molds that could be reconfigured or reused.

Left

Sequential Wall 2, ©Gramazio & Kohler, ETH Zürich. Constructed using additive digital fabrication methods, robots first cut and then stacked individual timber slats. The straight-edge timbers were positioned to create complex curved surfaces and to fulfill functional criteria (that the wall should be loadbearing, insulating, and waterproofing).

15. Material sources and resources

Materials libraries are an important resource for the designer; they may be part of a practice office (a "private" collection), or an external resource housed by a specialist company or an independent association (a semiprivate or public collection). Online libraries and databases are also becoming increasingly popular, and trade fairs and exhibitions provide excellent opportunities for encountering new and innovative materials.

Practice libraries (private)

In practice offices, materials are often kept in libraries, which vary in their formality—from drawers and boxes of samples roughly organized by type to carefully cataloged and arranged collections that can be searched using a database.

Technical information and data from manufacturers is a vital accompaniment to the physical material sample and forms an important part of the library. Other key information sources that may be kept in a materials library include trade directories and trade journals, which cover every conceivable product and material category from contract flooring to non-woven textiles.

Designers might employ a materials consultant, a materials librarian, or materials researcher to work on a specific project brief, or to oversee the organization of their materials library.

Above
Visitors consulting with a specialist advisor at the 100% Design fair, London, 2011.

Right
In practice, samples can be stored in managed libraries or more informally on shelves, in boxes, or on a samples table.

University/institutional libraries (semiprivate or public)

Some universities and other public institutions with materials libraries offer access to designers, though this may be limited through membership schemes or to alumni.

These institutional libraries often have a particular focus, such as the history of plastic materials, sustainable and environmentally friendly materials, metals, or perhaps materials that are relevant to a particular place or indigenous group of people.

The Construction Specifications Institute (CSI) publishes MasterFormat, a North American industry list of standardized numbers and titles for organizing construction bidding and contract requirements, specifications, drawing notes, cost data, and building operations.

In the United States, the School of Architecture at the University of Texas, Austin, has a materials library (both a physical archive and an electronic database) with over 25,000 samples. Similar archives exist at Harvard University's Graduate School of Design, the Rhode Island School of Design, and the Material ConneXion materials archive at Kendall College of Art and Design.[5]

In addition to materials kept in a library, many other resources can be used to develop designers' understanding of materials and introduce them to new material products. Some examples are listed on this page.

Materials databases

Databases provide access to a broad range of materials information. Some of the classification problems discussed above can be effectively addressed when working digitally, as materials can be tagged with multiple keywords relating to their physical and sensory properties as well as their intended applications. Links to manufacturers' websites, and to examples of the material in use can help you quickly understand what the material's properties and appropriate applications are.

One of the main drawbacks of a digital database is that it is very difficult to get an accurate idea of a material by looking at photographs and reading about it. Designers need to get their hands on the real thing in order to understand and make decisions about it; therefore, online resources should be seen as a complementary research tool, not a replacement for a physical library of material samples.

The companies behind the main online databases also have physical materials libraries, combining their offer of a virtual search tool, accessible from anywhere in the world, with the hands-on experience that real samples provide.

Materia, based in the Netherlands, comprises a physical resource center and a free online database: *Material Explorer*. Searches can be conducted using keywords, or by selecting from a range of different properties (including glossiness, texture, and translucence) as well as country of origin.
http://www.materia.nl (accessed 04.07.11)

matériO has libraries in Paris, Antwerp, and Barcelona, with future plans to open in Prague and Bratislava. Their subscription-based online database, *Materiotheque*, holds information on materials produced by more than 4,000 manufacturers.
http://www.materio.com (accessed 04.07.11)

Material ConneXion has libraries in New York, Bangkok, Cologne, Milan, Daegu (South Korea), Istanbul and Beijing. Their subscription-based online database covers an ever-growing range of materials.
http://www.materialconnexion.com (accessed 04.07.11)

Material Lab is a materials showroom located in London and established specifically as a resource for designers—"not a shop but a studio."
http://www.material-lab.co.uk (accessed 04.07.11)

5 Alison Zingaro, "Innovation in the Classroom," at http://materialconnexion.com/Home/Matter/MATTERMagazine/InnovationintheClassroom/tabid/751/Default.aspx (accessed 26.10.11).

Below left and right
matériO in Paris (left) and Materia Inspiration Center, Amsterdam (right). At such a resource, designers can be inspired by new materials or search for materials for a specific project.

Bottom
Materials Lab, London. Similar to the Materia Inspiration Center, this is a resource where designers can find out about the latest material trends and innovations and seek expert advice.

Trade fairs, exhibitions, manufacturers' showrooms

Trade fairs and exhibitions provide good opportunities to see a large range of different materials and products in one place. Manufacturers will often use these as a platform to launch a new product or announce an innovation. They also provide a forum for face-to-face discussion with technical sales representatives, who are usually very knowledgeable about what their materials can do and how they may be used. Manufacturers' showrooms can also be helpful—especially if you know the type of material you are looking for, or you need to get hold of samples very quickly.

International expositions and exhibitions include:

Six Cities Design Festival, all areas, Scotland, UK (January)

Toronto International Design Festival, Toronto, Canada (January)

Indian Design Festival, Pune, India (February)

Milan Furniture Fair and Public Design Festival, Milan, Italy (April)

Design Festa, Tokyo, Japan (May)

International Contemporary Furniture Fair (ICFF), New York, USA (May)

Interzum, Cologne, Germany (May)

DWELL on Design, Los Angeles, USA (June)

Architectural Biennale, Venice, Italy (June)

Istanbul Design Weekend, Istanbul, Turkey (June)

DMY International Design Festival, Berlin, Germany (June)

State of Design Festival, Melbourne, Australia (July)

Sydney Design, Sydney, Australia (August)

Copenhagen Design Week, Copenhagen, Denmark (August)

London Design Festival, London, UK (September)

Green Design Festival, Athens, Greece (September)

ZOW, Istanbul, Turkey (September)

Experimenta Design, Lisbon, Portugal (September)

World Design Congress, Beijing, China (October)

Bangkok Design Festival, Bangkok, Thailand (October)

IIDEX/NeoCon, Toronto, Canada (September/October)

Singapore Design Festival, Singapore (November)

Below left
The Material Sourcing Company's stand at Surface Design Show, London 2010.

Below
100% Design, London, 2011. Exhibitions and trade fairs provide opportunities for designers to see new products and materials and to speak to manufacturers and suppliers; material samples can also be collected for personal or practice-based materials libraries.

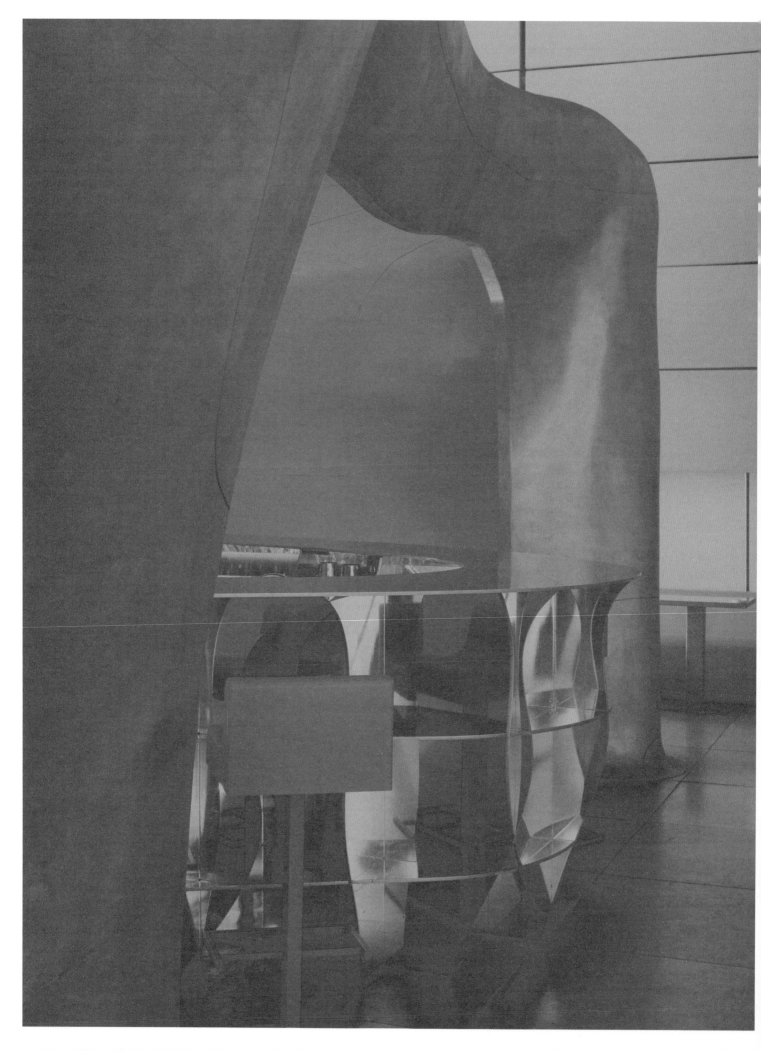

PART VI CASE STUDIES

Case study 1 Atmosphere
Beijing Noodle Bar, Las Vegas, Nevada, USA
Design Spirits Co. Ltd

An essence makes a space.
We search for that essence, to create a space
with long life.
As craftsmen, this is our design spirit.
Design Spirits

Design Spirits Co. Ltd is an interior design and
consultancy practice based in Tokyo. The Beijing
Noodle Bar, in Caesars Palace, Las Vegas, was
designed by Yuhkichi Kawai of Design Spirits in
collaboration with graphic designer Alan Chan and
lighting designer Kazuhika Suzuki of Muse-D Co.

Located in a huge hotel and adjacent
to a casino, the restaurant has a very
distinctive, ephemeral atmosphere created
through a veneer of material and light. It is
an oasis of calm, a retreat from the noisy
gaming machines and neon lights.

Design Spirits' concept for the interior was
to cover the space with light diffused through
a silk-like skin. The practice's aim was to move
away from the conventional elements that

This page
Clockwise from top left: the fish tank-
lined entrance corridor, main dining area,
and banquette seating on the side.

define an interior—such as walls, floors, and ceilings—and to create an interior with seamless borders: a single entity. The range and quantity of materials is minimized and a single decorative motif, an arabesque pattern, is used throughout to create a cohesive, harmonious whole.

Upon entry, customers move through an enclosed entrance of sparkling aquarium tanks, which provides a transition from the noisy, aggressive atmosphere of the casino to the calmer, tranquil interior of the restaurant.

The arabesque pattern is repeated at different scales: white built-in furniture is etched with the pattern, and laser-cut white powder-coated steel sheets are used on the walls and ceilings and lit from behind with LED lights to cast arabesque patterns on the tables, chairs, and floor, creating a "soft, cocoon-like interior." All the loose furniture is white with details in stainless steel and aluminum; the only colors used in the interior are pink, which gives a gentle warm blush to the room, and flashes of orange from the aquarium fish.

The composition of materials is elegant and restrained, and Design Spirits' aim of creating a tranquil retreat has been achieved; the practice describes the atmosphere created as: "a sensuous embrace like the wonder of a deep forest or the secrets of an ocean."

1 Entrance
2 Front kitchen
3 Semiprivate dining
4 Fish tank
5 Service station
6 Main kitchen

Right and below
Drawings are used extensively by Design Spirits to develop and refine their designs and communicate with their clients.

Case study 2 Brand identity

Projects for Levi Strauss International, Florence, Tokyo, Berlin
Jump Studios

Jump Studios is a London-based practice that aims to achieve innovation by breaking down barriers between creative disciplines —its creative team includes design consultants, architects, interior designers, graphic designers, and digital designers.

The practice specializes in architecture, interior design, brand consultancy, and installations/design projects that are underpinned by clear concepts, taking "intangible ideas, such as brands, and creating tangible, physical spaces."[1] When working on a project it follows the principle of the "Three Es," all of which have relevance when considering and selecting materials:

- Efficiency: plan, program, budget, resources
- Engagement: to consider how the user or client will engage with a space
- Expression: to respond to, or create, a visual identity for the client

Jump Studios' projects for Levi Strauss provide good examples of how materials can been used to reinforce and communicate brand identity or to give visual expression to a client's image. Each project is different, but the Levi brand image is maintained in each location:

Below left
Levi Strauss, Pitti Immagine, Florence.

Below right
Levi's LVC Store, Tokyo.

Levi's Pitti Immagine, Florence

Jump Studios was commissioned by Levi Strauss Europe to design an exhibition space for the Florentine fashion trade fair Pitti Immagine that expressed the brand value of craftsmanship. By referring to the traditional couture atelier, a space in which "you will find one large table around which the garment-makers work, with their beautiful hand-crafted pieces hanging above the table, wrapped in tissue paper,"[2] Jump Studios designed an environment that evoked a traditional craft-centered fashion house:

The focal point of the exhibition was a cluster of antique wooden drawers, above which vintage denim jeans were suspended, wrapped in dressmaker's tissue and lit from above, creating a "ceiling" surface of delicate paper and tailored denim. New products were housed in the heavy wooden drawers, which were opened for the individual upon request, giving ritual and ceremony to the process of buying and heightening the perceived value of the crafted product.

The perimeter of the room was clad in mirrors, expanding and distorting the physical space and creating a sense of looking forward and backward. This concept was a "response to the paradox of the two premium Levi's brands: Levi's Vintage Collection (LVC) and Red. LVC focuses on the heritage and history of the company, while Red is the 'lab' where Levi's look to the future with new cuts and engineering."[3]

Levi's LVC Store, Tokyo

Jump Studios was commissioned by Levi Strauss Japan to design the first solo LVC (Levi's Vintage Collection) boutique worldwide. The site was a Japanese worker's cottage in the Aoyama area of Tokyo.

For this project, Jump Studios took its inspiration from a pair of worn Levi's jeans that have developed their "own unique material character over time"[4]—the shape of the wearer, faded denim, thinning fabric, frayed edges, etc. The concept that the inherent qualities of materials can be revealed by time was applied to this interior by using materials that also take on their own patina and character with use: untreated wooden cladding with copper details and a raw concrete floor that would be worn smooth. In contrast to these "unfinished" materials, the crafted products were placed like jewels in velvet lined, full-height drawers— conveying the message that Levi's products are collectable, desirable, and precious commodities.

1 http://www.jump-studios.com/#/about-us/what-we-do (accessed 04.07.11).
2 http://www.jump-studios.com/#/showcase/levis-pitti-immagine (accessed 04.07.11).
3 http://www.jump-studios.com/#/showcase/levis-pitti-immagine (accessed 04.07.11).
4 http://www.jump-studios.com/#/showcase/levis-lvc-store (accessed 04.07.11).

This page
Levi's 150, Berlin.

Levi's 150, Berlin

To celebrate the 150th anniversary of Levi Strauss, Jump Studios was asked to design an exhibition that described the history of Strauss as an emigrant from Germany to America and the significance of that journey to the company's success.

The exhibition was held in a disused railway station in Berlin, giving conceptual relevance and emotional resonance to the design. It was designed using the track as a timeline, marked with "billboards" that described stories and myths about the Levi Strauss brand.

The products themselves were contained within purpose-designed cargo train carriages, which were positioned within the industrial, cold environment of the disused station; finishes were deliberately weathered on the outside and the interiors were treated with highly "polished" materials such as perforated backlit copper and refined timber, to create a "magical and transformative experience once visitors crossed the threshold."[5] Like the drawers in Tokyo, the interiors of the carriages presented the merchandise as precious, gem-like commodities.

In each of these Levi projects, it is clear that materials have been selected to reinforce a brand identity: they have been used to represent ideas of heritage, tradition, craftsmanship, quality, and style. While each venue expresses a different concept or narrative, the values underpinning the brand remain constant and are reflected in the interior designs.

5   http://www.jump-studios.com/#/showcase/
    levis-150 (accessed 04.07.11).

Case study 3 Narratives

Collaborative interiors, various locations, London, UK

Tracey Neuls

Above left and right
Pop-up store and exhibition designed in
collaboration with Retrouvius, London, 2007.

Tracey Neuls is a shoe designer based in London whose interdisciplinary approach to design has resulted in a number of collaborative, innovative works, including various interior installations in her store on Brompton Road.

One of her first collaborative "pop-up" store designs with the reclamation company Retrouvius, open for only three weeks, adopted methods of re-appropriation in its design: discarded drawers (supplied by Retrouvius), once used to conceal and contain small objects, were assembled vertically, their interiors exposed, to create containment and enclosure at the scale of the room. The store was defined by these discarded drawers—the "retrieved" objects— giving the interior a material quality that could not be manufactured: worn timber, rusting hinges, burnished brass—materials that evoked memories of the past and a suggestion of lives lost. The drawers' reuse or "rebirth" provided both symbolic meaning and also a sustainable approach to using materials in interior design.

Tracey has also collaborated with contemporary artist Nina Saunders, and the British textiles company, Sanderson, in an event marking the latter's 150th anniversary.

This interior was centered around a "liquid," morphing chair designed by Saunders and a specially designed collection of shoes by Neuls: both designer and artist used reissued vintage Sanderson fabric in their installations, and both played with ideas of distortion and subverting conventions in their use of materials. The rubber soles of Neul's shoes were cast with Sanderson's textile, giving pattern to all sides of the shoe, and Saunders' chair, a piece of furniture that one would expect to be made of solid and secure materials, has a disconcerting disintegration of form.

The combination of Sanderson textiles, the amorphous chair, and the shoes suspended in a "decapitated" forest had a surreal quality; the juxtaposition of materials, pattern, and form disorientated the user as the boundaries between the real world and the world of dreams become blurred—the narrative is not explicit and the story is left to the viewer to complete.

Finally, for the London Design Festival 2010 Tracey collaborated with Nicola Yeoman, a London-based artist. In this installation, also at the Brompton Road store, materials were used to evoke the freedom and creativity of childhood play, and memories of making with found objects: buttons, beads, fabrics, and fastenings.

The installation distorts perspective, encouraging the user of the space to revisit the imaginative inner life of the child where the world beneath the table becomes the host of numerous alternative landscapes and narratives ... anything is possible.

All of Neuls' collaborative installations demonstrate a narrative use of materials and material objects, which tell their own stories but also leave the user of the space free to interpret their meaning.

Below left

Most Curious, a celebration of Sanderson's 150th anniversary; pop-up store and exhibition, London.

Below and bottom

Home, an installation for London Design Festival 2010; pop-up store and exhibition.

Case study 4 Pattern and surface

Installations, Sweden

Gunilla Klingberg

Gunilla Klingberg is an artist living and working in Sweden. She creates colorful and highly decorative installations using surface and pattern. However, these installations are more than mere spectacle: the seductive interiors, installations, paintings, and graphic designs provide a commentary on global commercialization, geopolitical issues, and consumerism.

In many of her works, Gunilla combines corporate logos, everyday signs, and the symbols that saturate our environment to create new imagery. The new designs reference Oriental artwork and the sacred mandalas of Hinduism and Buddhism; they juxtapose Eastern and Western conventions, the spiritual and the prosaic, the commercial and the religious, and they convey messages of both hope and despair:

I employ symbols that are visible in everyday life. The logotypes and brands I use are neither glamorous nor "loaded" brands like Nike, which we tend to—after Naomi Klein's "No Logo"—more easily recognize as something "evil" because of their horrible production conditions, with child labor, sweatshops.[1]

The materials selected for Gunilla's designs are usually simple everyday materials or objects presented in a new way, for example the

scaffolding and self-adhesive tape printed with logos and symbols used in *Cosmic Matter*, the kitchen cabinets in *Split Vision,* and the screen-printed linoleum and vinyl film in *Repeat Pattern*. In these examples, the substance is secondary to the materials' surface treatment: the pattern and decoration applied to the material.

The use of the everyday, both in her use of materials and of graphic signs and symbols, is an important aspect of Gunilla's artworks:

Each work is built up with the more unglamorous design of everyday life, which in turn makes it very simple for the observer to find his or her own position in—and connection to—the space. [2]

Reimagining and reconfiguring familiar objects and imagery, and understanding that materials and their surfaces can convey meaning, is an important skill of the interior designer: materials may be applied as a "veneer," but the "veneer" can have intellectual substance.

1   http://www.gunillaklingberg.com/text.Pernille.
    html, Quote 4 (accessed 29.11.11).
2   Mats Stjernstedt at http://www.gunillaklingberg.
    com (accessed 04.07.11).

Above left
Repeat Pattern, 2004.

Above right
Split Vision bathroom cabinets, 2010.

Below left and bottom
Cosmic Matter: scaffolding, printed tape, highly
polished metal, wall paintings, 2009.

Below
Brand New View, 2003.

Case study 5 Creating space

softwall + softblock modular systems

molo design, ltd

Molo, based in Vancouver, Canada, is a collaborative design and production studio led by Stephanie Forsythe, Todd MacAllen, and Robert Pasut. The molo studio is dedicated to research in materials and the exploration of space making. As a design and manufacturing company, it creates and distributes its unique and innovative products to clients around the world. Molo products grow from Forsythe and MacAllen's architectural explorations. Inspired by the idea that smaller tactile objects have a real potency in the physical experience of space, the practice sets out to create objects that define intimate temporal spaces.

Molo's products have received numerous international awards and have been acquired by museums and galleries worldwide, including the Museum of Modern Art in New York. The project "softwall + softblock" is a modular space-shaping system at the core of molo's "soft" collection. Utilizing flexible honeycomb structures that expand, contract, and flex, forming sculptural spaces and seating topographies, "soft" is a

research-driven exploration of materials, structure, and space making. The elements of the "soft" collection have been designed to be uniquely shaped for a specific occasion or space, folded away for storage and/or reshaped again in variable and dynamic ways, replacing inflexible alternatives for partitioning and arranging space.

The tactile, experiential qualities of the textile-and-kraft-paper softwall + softblock system are suited to shaping intimate ephemeral areas within larger, open spaces. Softwall + softblock further provides a medium for shaping the acoustics and lighting of a space. The cellular structure and vertical pleats that run the course of its expanded walls serve to dampen sound, while translucent or opaque versions of softwall + softblock can sculpt the light in a space.

Molo's new system of flexible LED lighting, which integrates with its existing softwall + softblock modular systems, transforms these elements into completely flexible, freestanding, glowing partitions. This luminous version of softwall + softblock emphasizes the visual

delicacy of the translucent white textile fiber and makes the expansion, contraction, and fluid movement of these freestanding, soft structures all the more magical. And now, the element of light, softly glowing and contained within the flowing layers of softwall + softblock, can bring another expression and atmosphere to dim, moody environments: spaces created to immerse themselves in the dusky shadows of twilight and night. As a light source, softwall + softblock provides the possibility to shape pure, uncluttered sculptural environments using softwalls, softseating, and softlighting.

Opening softwall is dramatic experience, as the honeycomb expands to create a completely freestanding structure, hundreds of times larger than its compressed form. You can choose to open any softwall or softblock element to a maximum 14 ft 9 in in length, or opt to open it a shorter length to suit a particular occasion or space. The softwall + softblock modular system includes a variety of standard and custom heights, up to 10 ft.

Opposite
The textile system is made of a non-woven polyethylene material (trade name Tyvek®). It is 100% recyclable and is made from 5–15% recycled content. Its lightweight paper look and feel is tear-, UV-, and water-resistant, making it durable to handle and maintain.

Below, left column
The flexible, freestanding partition system can expand and contract to shape intimate spaces within larger open areas. The cellular structure dampens sound while sculpting the light of a space in different ways, depending on whether the opaque or translucent version of the system is being used.

Below, right column
There is also a version of the system featuring integrated LED lighting, which turns the white textile volume into an amazing source of light. The luminous version of the system emphasizes the visual delicacy of the textile fiber.

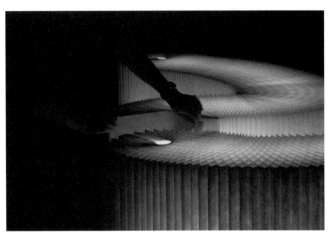

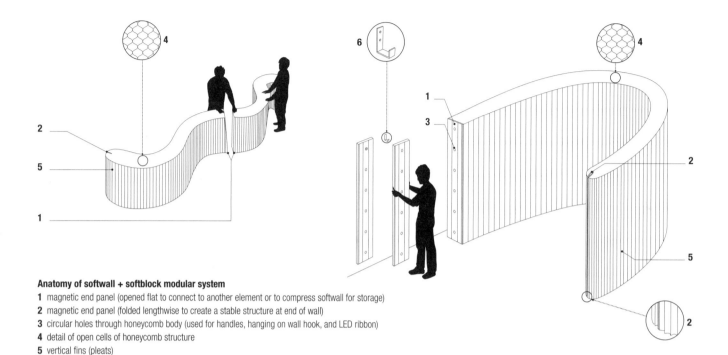

Anatomy of softwall + softblock modular system

1 magnetic end panel (opened flat to connect to another element or to compress softwall for storage)
2 magnetic end panel (folded lengthwise to create a stable structure at end of wall)
3 circular holes through honeycomb body (used for handles, hanging on wall hook, and LED ribbon)
4 detail of open cells of honeycomb structure
5 vertical fins (pleats)
6 stainless steel wall hook (for storage)

The system's elements are available in two materials: textile and kraft paper. The former is a 100 percent polyethylene non-woven textile with a lightweight paper-like look and feel. It is highly tear-, UV-, and water-resistant, and thus easy to handle and maintain. softwall + softblock is available in translucent white and opaque black. Light transmitting through a white textile softwall element brings the visually delicate fibers of the material to life, absorbing and containing luminosity in a similar way to a block of snow. The opaque, black softwall is dyed a deep, rich, inky black with UV-resistant bamboo-charcoal ink, which produces a subtle sheen reminiscent of charred wood and allows the fine pattern of the fibers to show.

The second material, kraft paper, is an unbleached paper made with 50 percent recycled fiber and 50 percent new, long fiber. The new, long fibers give strength, reinforcing the smaller recycled fibers to make a stiff robust paper. Kraft paper softwall + softblock elements are all opaque and available in a natural, unbleached brown with a warm, earthy presence, and also a deep black that has been dyed with bamboo-charcoal ink.

Assembly

All elements in the softwall + softblock modular system connect together with concealed magnets in an almost seamless way, with the vertical joints between elements blending with the rhythm of the vertically pleated structures. The magnetic end panels can also anchor to any steel or magnetic surface. A white powder-coated steel strip is available from molo to create an anchor point on walls, columns, or cabinets.

The "soft" collection combines abstractly poetic, sculptural form and pragmatic function to create spaces for modern flexible life.

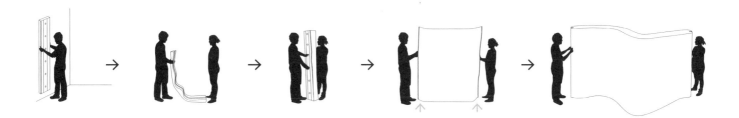

Above

The softwall is easy for two people to assemble. The folded wall is first lifted off of its wall storage unit. While continuing to hold opposing end panels by their circular holes, pull the softwall open by slightly lifting the ends off the floor (to reduce friction) and then slowly moving away from one another until the wall is pulled open about 10 ft.

Below

Softblocks may be stacked in horizontal layers to reach a desired height. Set up the first layer of softblocks, connecting blocks end to end, folding the magnetic end panels lengthwise for stability. The panels can then be arranged to the desired configuration before starting on the next layer.

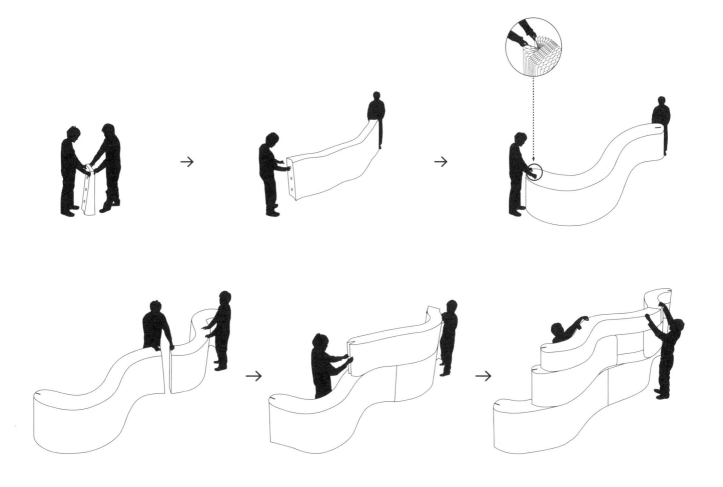

Case study 6 A material response to site
Concept for a temporary installation in a church, Lybster, Scotland, UK
Alex Hoare

Alex Hoare is an artist and a scenographer. The following "design journal" describes her investigation of and response to a site, its alternative readings, histories, and narratives, and ultimately her material response.

Scenography
"My first impressions of the exterior of the building were of an imposing and unwelcoming façade, a shell to protect the inhabitant from the Scottish weather. The interior looked dark and empty from the outside.

On entering, my initial impression was of a damp and cold space, the earthy smell of wet and decay, cold air, the sound of swallows singing and flitting through rafters, and bright light from the windows piercing the dim interior. Observing the rest of the group filing through the door, like tourists with their cameras, my thoughts turned to the past, of other people funneling through the door, down a central aisle and into the pews (now gone but which must have once existed). I imagined singing, preaching, and the church as a haven from the inclement weather, the sea, and the harshness of life in a fishing village. I walked through the space as the communities of the past may have done."

Visual stimulus
"Several things struck me about the visual appearance of the building. Firstly, the structure of the gallery/balcony, which indicated there may have been side aisles, adding to the path of my imagined flow of people through the space. The design of the windows also mirrored a sort of funneling effect.

Overall, I came away from the first visit with a sense that the building was a quiet place of refuge. The inside was a dark space where you were drawn toward the light from the windows; the solidity of the architecture contrasted with the fragility and decay of the interior."

Place
"The community's historical relationship to the sea played an important part in the development of my ideas. Life as a fisherman in the 19th century and into the 20th was very hard. The constant proximity to the elements (sea, wind, rain, rock) and the nature of their work must have meant that the precariousness of life was daily apparent. Reading and listening to oral histories from the Am Baile website highlighted the importance of the relationship to the sea and the herring fishing industry.[1] Bachelard states, in *The Poetics of Space*: "A nest-house is never young ... not only

Above far left
Setting up the installation.

Above center and right
Inspirational photographs of local fishermen, fishing net, and the church window.

Below
Inspirational photographs of the waterfront area.

Bottom
Composite visualization of the project.

Below
Detail of the glass curtain.

do we come back to it, but we dream of coming back to it, the way a bird comes back to its nest, or a lamb to the fold."[2] This quote summed up my imagining of fishermen returning from the sea to the village, the hearth, the church, and perceptions of the space in a metaphorical sense.

My extended observations of the place incorporated walks down the coast and in the next village, Latheronwheel. Visual motifs kept repeating themselves: the way the sea channeled through the rocks, the river rushed over the stones finding a way through, a sense of movement, and again "funneling." The colors of the water, the kelp, and the sky were everywhere, steel blues, amber browns, light aqua pools—I started to think about these qualities in relation to the building and to the material I had chosen to work with, glass.

The colors of the natural environment, and its direct relationship with the community that would have used the church led me to start experimenting with glass to achieve watery effects, encapsulating movement and light in small segments that could be strung together to create a curtain. For some time I have wanted to experiment with the idea of an articulated curtain of glass, to try and create a wall of light and color. My initial experiments using clear glass focused on methods to string the glass together.

At around this time I met a retired fisherman in the village who agreed to teach me to make nets. Whilst in the Waterfront Museum in Lybster, I had noticed a visual display of a net which formed in channels, and that in photos of Lybster from the past, nets are apparent everywhere, hanging out to dry. They are still omnipresent in the harbor today, although in the form of lobster pots rather than fishing nets. I chose to integrate the netting into the glass to hold it and make it hang but also to show the nets hanging in the water."

Final concept

"The final concept is for a temporary, walk-through installation to be located in the church during the transitional phase from derelict building to new arts center in the village. The installation will use curtains of glass to divide the space into channels. It is intended as a temporary installation and will include soundscapes of the external environment, i.e. sea, birds, waves. A bench, with integrated headphones, will run around the sides of the room so that visitors can pause at different points to listen to the stories of the old inhabitants of the village relating different facets of life in the village.

The color in the glass curtain will change as the visitor moves around the space, and the glass will reflect the changing light as the day progresses, so different places will be illuminated at different times of the day.

In addition to this, there will be an oral history booth at the side of the entrance porch where people can record their memories and stories, and people will be encouraged to place rolled up notes into the glass netted curtain with ideas of how they would like the space to be used in the future."
Alex Hoare, 2011

1   http://www.ambaile.org.uk (accessed 04.07.11).
2   Gaston Bachelard, *The Poetics of Space*, Boston: Beacon Press, 1994, p. 99.

Case study 7 Sustainable exhibition design

"Atmosphere: Exploring Climate Science," Science Museum, London, UK

Casson Mann

Exhibition design has evolved to become a very influential and specialist branch of interior design. Beginning perhaps with Renaissance "cabinets of curiosities" and their equivalents across the globe, exhibition design has become established as a sophisticated form of spatial design that is informed by the fields of curation and museology, and developments in product design, materials science, and technological innovations. Exhibitions are no longer simply "contained" collections of objects, but can be dynamic, interactive spaces that provide education and recreation, information and spectacle. An exhibition can be contained within a room or series of rooms but might also occupy much bigger spaces—consider "installations" at world fairs, expos, and events such as the Venice Biennale.

Casson Mann are recognized for their distinctive interiors and particularly for their work in museums and galleries. When designing the exhibition "Atmosphere: Exploring Climate Science" for the Science Museum in London in 2010, they were concerned that the materials they used should satisfy both functional and aesthetic considerations but that they should also specify materials from sustainable sources with minimal impact on the environment.

The physical construction of the exhibition was thought to be responsible for around 40 percent of the lifetime climate change impact of the whole project; only a small proportion of this was estimated to come from the emissions embodied in the materials. Nevertheless, the choice of materials offered the possibility to support emerging low-carbon construction technology and to provide visual evidence (to visitors) of practical carbon management.

Several materials were considered for the floor, walls, ceiling, and table displays. These included plywood, oriented strand board (OSB) or "Flakeboard," "Ecosheet," acrylic/plaster sheeting, Corian® surfacing product, Formica, polystyrene blockwork, fiberglass, honeycomb cardboard panels, and reusable scaffolding. The materials were assessed for their functionality, cost, and broader environmental credentials, as well as their embedded carbon.

Following consideration, Ecosheet emerged

Above

The main element of the display units is provided by continuous folding sheets of FSB plywood.

as a particularly interesting new material, made from recycled mixed plastic waste. It was thought important to support this new material if possible, so the decision was taken to use it in a small area of the exhibition where it could be a practical demonstration of a sustainable technology and its long-term functionality could be tested.

The "Tectonic Plates" feature of the display was conceived as a single continuous folding sheet material that would provide the principal support for all of the exhibits. Though Ecosheet was given a considerable amount of attention during design development, FSB plywood emerged as the safest option in terms of having a well-established history of fabrication techniques and durability that would ensure the structures lasted the lifetime of the gallery. On a schedule of materials issued to Casson Mann by the Crichton Carbon Centre, plywood and softwood also rated well and achieved a

Left and above
A delicate fabric ceiling follows the patterns of isobars.

low CO_2e/unit score. Softwood and plywood formers were, therefore, used to create the undulating forms and associated structures. These materials were finished in a tough polyester lacquer—a robust finish that added color and could be used as a projection surface.

In other areas of the exhibition timber was chosen for its natural, warm, tactile quality. Spruce, supplied by the specialist timber contractor Eurban, was specified because it had particularly good credentials as a fast-growing timber from well-managed sources. Eurban also have a preference for integrated sawmill manufacturing plants local to the UK. The Eurban sheets were cross-laminated and bonded with non-formaldehyde adhesives.

The selection of materials has resulted in an interior that is both "responsible" in its specification and visually engaging. Color is used to create a harmonious purple-blue-green background which is punctuated by complementary yellow and orange, used to signify points of information and interaction. The luminance of the delicate fabric ceiling, which follows the patterning of isobars, shrouds the interior.

Case study 8 Material detail and construction I

Pink Bar, Pompidou Center, Paris, France

Jakob + MacFarlane

Using digital technologies, Jakob + MacFarlane designed Georges Restaurant and the later insertion, Pink Bar, to occupy the top floor of the Pompidou Center in Paris.

The host building, designed by Richard Rogers and Renzo Piano in the High-Tech style, was organized according to a 31½ in structural grid that was also used to locate ceilings, floors, and services. The internal services were exposed and color coded: yellow for electricity, blue for air, and green for water.

Jakob + MacFarlane were not able to alter the existing building and could only connect the new structures to the floor (not walls or ceilings). Their intention was to create an insertion with a distinctive identity but that also responded conceptually to the character of the site. The total floor area of the project is 322 sq ft.

Their approach was to use the existing grid as a generator for forms that appeared to emerge from the gridded floor but which then "exploded" and transformed to create morphed forms.

The insertions were manufactured by a boat-building company who were able to transfer skills normally applied to yacht and ship construction. Monocoque structures were adopted—these utilized the strength of the ³⁄₁₆ in thick aluminum panels that were used for both the floor and as the cladding/structure of the organic forms. The aluminum surfaces were brushed to both absorb and reflect light. The internal surfaces of the new insertions were lined with thin, brightly colored sheet rubber.

Pink Bar is built inside one of the original monocoque forms created for the restaurant. The form of the bar is also based on the same grid as the original restaurant, but instead of deforming the grid to create the surfaced volumes, Jakob + MacFarlane "carved out" a resultant volume from a three-dimensional matrix of 0.024 cu in, a micro-division of the original building grid at the Pompidou Center. This matrix is built from ³⁄₈ in thick aluminum sheets using laser-cutting technology.

The cuboid furniture for Pink Bar was also designed by Jakob + MacFarlane and produced by Capellini. Lighting was designed by iGuzzini.

Below left and right
The bar was installed in one of the restaurant's original aluminum-clad monocoque structures.

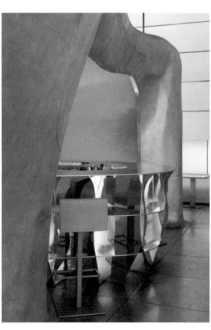

Right
Part plan showing the bar area.

Below
Sections through the monocoque bar structure.

Bottom left
The Pink Bar was constructed off-site using ⅜ in thick laser-cut aluminum sheets (in this image, the aluminum is protected by a layer of plastic). The conceptual "grid" or matrix (which relates to the Pompidou's structural grid) is clearly visible.

Bottom right
The organic, "blobular" forms designed for Georges Restaurant were constructed by a boat-building company. This image shows the aluminum monocoque structure (with metal ribs and 3⁄16 in thick sheets of aluminum) being assembled.

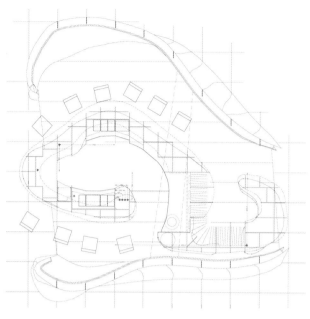

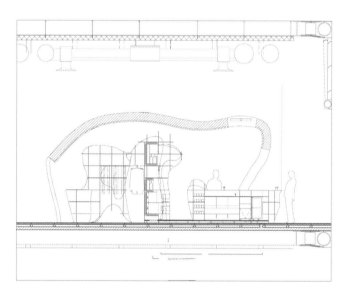

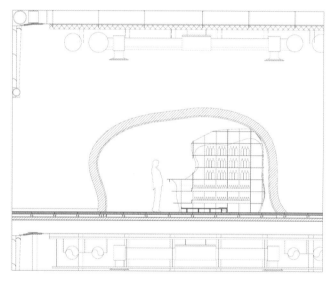

Case study 9 Material detail and construction II

Republic of Fritz Hansen staircase, London, UK

BDP (concept and design) and TinTab (detail and construction)

The initial site consisted of two floor levels, which needed to be combined not only to unite the two spaces but also to enhance the light, views, and connectivity between them. The creation of the opening and design of the staircase were largely informed by these considerations.

A series of studies were carried out to determine the best position and geometry in terms of maximizing the opening and the creation of a structure that appeared to float in the space. This was achieved in consultation with the client and through the use of simple three-dimensional representations.

The initial inspiration for the staircase came from a series designed by Arne Jacobsen (who designed several of Fritz Hansen's iconic products), notably that for the Danmarks Nationalbank completed in

Above and left
The stove-enameled main framework gives a sense of strength, while the glass balustrade creates a feeling of lightness.

Above
The staircase under construction.

Right
Detail construction drawings and section.

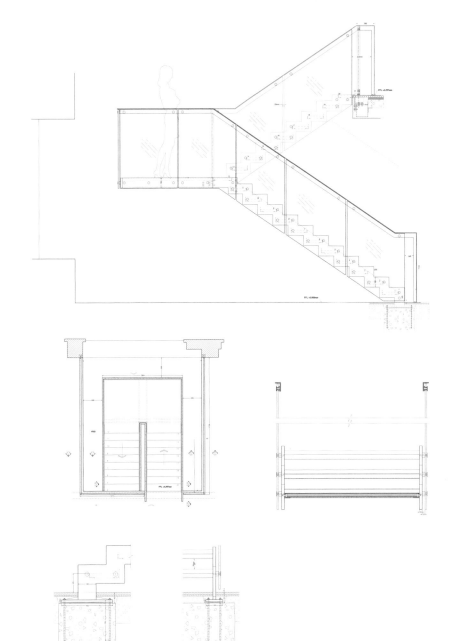

1978, together with a desire to create a robust, industrially crafted element that would feel part of the original building.

The materials were chosen to reflect these aspirations and also to meet budget considerations. The stove-enameled main framework and uprights provide a strong aesthetic, with the stepped stringer providing a reference to the Jacobsen heritage. Within this a structural glass balustrade creates a feeling of lightness capped with a simple angle-section handrail. Glass fixings are in a bronze finish to create a subtle link to the general palette of finishes. Slabs of Multiply flooring finished in oak veneer for the main treads add a natural element and link the finishes of the upper and lower floors.

Of particular note is the extended landing, which allows both for social gathering and the potential for display areas. This created some structural challenges, which necessitated the use of a product called "Z steel," which provides an enhanced structural performance, allowing the design sections to be maintained at the desired proportions.

Text provided by Stephen Anderson, Interior Design Director, BDP

Conclusion

Like the artist, the designer has a palette of materials that can be composed and constructed to create surface and form, to represent a concept, to express an identity, to engage the senses, and to elicit a response (physical, emotional, or intellectual) from the audience or user. Unlike most artists (there are exceptions), the designer also has to consider the functional application of materials and respond to the needs of the client and the occupants whose lives will be impacted by the choices made: staff and patients in hospitals, curators and visitors to museums, staff and pupils in schools, actors and audience, retailers and consumers, residents of homes, etc.

The opportunities for designers and their use of materials are many and varied, and the associated responsibilities are significant. At the beginning of this book, we stated that the designer must be able to assess the aesthetic and functional properties of materials while maintaining an ethical, investigative, and innovative approach to design; designers' attitudes toward these considerations will inform their actions:

Ethical attitude designers' ethical positions will inform many of their choices regarding materials, choices that ultimately impact on the well-being of people, animals, and the environment. A responsible attitude will help to improve health and safety (of material providers, manufacturers, construction workers, and users), and the sustainability and diversity of resources.

Investigative attitude engaged and inquiring designers will seek information and record their observations of the natural and synthetic world. They will be inquisitive about historical and contemporary practices (within their own discipline and beyond); they will collect samples and will ask questions, challenge answers, and as a result increase their knowledge and understanding of materials.

Innovative attitude armed with knowledge and understanding, the designer can experiment with materials, interpret the practice of other disciplines, and test alternative methods of applying, juxtaposing, and assembling materials. This attitude is one of invention and progression.

Adopting positive attitudes will give rigor and integrity to the designer's actions—actions that could improve well-being and result in interiors that are exemplary and inspirational in their aesthetic, technical, and functional use of materials.

Left

In their design for the London Issey Miyake store (1988), Stanton Williams created an interior with a lasting quality. A restrained palette of materials—including oak, bead-blasted stainless steel, powder-coated stainless steel, glass, render, and limestone—was selected and composed to created an environment that complemented the clothing on display. The architects have expressed material qualities and material interfaces, articulating joints and junctions, fixings and fastenings. Note the use of negative details, shadow gaps, and the way in which some materials wrap around others.

Below

More than 20 years later, in 2011, Stanton Williams completed their design for the new campus for Central Saint Martins College of Art at King's Cross in London. The design combines a historic 19th-century granary building and transit sheds with a 656-ft long new building. In the historic buildings, existing materials and components such as the timber structure and sliding industrial doors were preserved—the marks of previous occupants are visible and the buildings' histories can be "read." New insertions are restrained and composed to provide a subtle contrast with existing materials; material interfaces and new services are expressed and clearly articulated—an honest approach to the use of materials in an existing building.

Glossary

assemblage In art, the placing together of found objects to create two- or three-dimensional compositions.

BREEAM The UK Building Research Establishment's Environmental Assessment Method sets the standard for best practice in sustainable building design, construction, and operation and measures a building's environmental performance.

biomimicry The process of taking inspiration from nature and applying observations to design solutions.

carcinogenic Term for any substance that causes cancer.

chiaroscuro The distribution of light and shade or dramatic tonal contrast in a painting or drawing.

chord The simultaneous sounding of a group of musical notes, usually three or more in number.

collage In art, a composition made from a collection of elements (paper, text, found images, photographs, etc.) assembled to create a new whole.

color In art, term referring to hue (red, blue, green, etc.) as distinct from other formal elements such as tone, pattern, shape, and line.

composite Term to describe synthetic or naturally occurring materials made from two or more material elements.

composition In the visual arts, the arrangement and proportion of elements in relation to each other.

CAD (computer-aided design) Technology used to create and represent or document designs.

CAM (computer-aided manufacturing) Technology used to control machines or robots to manufacture physical objects (linked to **CAD**).

CNC (computer numerical control) Automated machinery linked to **CAD** and **CAM** systems and used to create physical objects.

counterpoint In music, two or more melodies or parts performed simultaneously; the parts have harmonic relationships but may have different rhythms and contours.

dichroic Term used to describe optical properties in glass that allow an array of apparently changing colors to be displayed.

discord In music, a lack of harmony or dissonance, a disharmonic mingling of sounds.

ductile Term for a malleable material that has plasticity in tension.

durable Able to resist wear and decay; long-lasting.

eco-efficient Term for goods created using fewer resources with the intention of slowing the depletion of resources and the emission of polluting chemicals.

empirical Knowledge derived from observation, experimentation, or experience as opposed to theory.

fabric In architectural design, fashion, and textiles, the material used to create form.

fragile Easily broken, delicate, or brittle.

intervention In architectural design, an insertion or change made to an existing place or space.

iridescent Quality whereby surfaces appear to change color when the viewing angle or angle of illumination is shifted.

LEED The Leadership of Energy and Environmental Design, the United States Green Building Council's (**USGBC**) points rating system for buildings that adhere to a green footprint.

mutagenic An agent that can cause changes in genetic material resulting in mutations (including cancer).

objective Based on facts, not influenced by personal bias or opinions; the opposite of subjective.

ocularcentrism The state of vision being privileged over the other senses.

opacity The degree to which an object allows light to pass through. An opaque object does transmit light.

palette In the visual arts and architectural design, the selection of colors, materials, textures, etc., composed to create the artwork or space.

parti sketch The overarching concept for a scheme expressed in a simple or abstracted drawing.

polymer A synthetic material formed by a process of molecular linkage, by which large chains of monomers form a molecule with a repeated structural unit. Examples include plastics and rubber.

proprioception A sense of the body's relationship to and position in space.

readymade (or found art) The repositioning or reconfiguring of existing everyday objects (not previously considered to be art).

resilient Not easily transformed or able to return to its original form after some degree of bending, stretching, pressing, etc.

sensory Of or relating to the senses; experience gained through one or more senses.

synthetic Man-made rather than naturally occurring.

tone In the visual arts, the gradation of light and dark.

transient An experience, idea, or image that is short-lasting or temporary.

translucency The degree to which some light passes through a material; the diffusion of light.

transparency The property of a material that allows light to be transmitted. Although clear, a transparent material may be colored.

USGBC The United States Green Building Council.

Further reading

Abercrombie, S., *A Philosophy of Interior Design*, Harper and Row, New York, 1990

Anderson, J., Shiers, D., and Sinclair, M., *The Green Guide to Specification*, third edition, Wiley-Blackwell, Oxford, 2002

Ashby, M., and Johnson, K., *Materials and Design: The Art and Science of Material Selection in Product Design*, Butterworth-Heinemann, Oxford, 2010

Ballard Bell, V., *Materials for Architectural Design,* Laurence King, London, 2006

Aynsley, J., Breward, C., and Kwint, M., eds, *Material Memories: Design and Evocation,* Berg, Oxford, 1999

Baard, E., "Unbreakable" in *Architecture*, June 2001

Berge, B., *The Ecology of Building Materials*, Architectural Press, Oxford, 2009

Beylerian, G., and Dent, A., *Material Connexion*, Thames & Hudson, London, 2005

Beylerian, G., and Dent, A., *Ultra Materials: How Materials Innovation is Changing the World*, first edition, Thames & Hudson, London, 2007

Beylerian, G., *Material Strategies: Innovative Applications in Architecture*, Princeton Architectural Press, New York, 2012

Braungart, M., and McDonough, W., *Cradle to Cradle: Remaking the way we make things*, Vintage, London, 2009

Brooker, G., and Stone, S., *Re-readings: Interior Architecture and the Design Principles of Remodelling Existing Buildings*, RIBA Publishing, London, 2004

Brooker, G., and Stone, S., *Form and Structure*, AVA, Lausanne, 2007

Brownell, B., ed., *Transmaterial: A Catalog of Materials that Redefine our Physical Environment*, Princeton Architectural Press, New York, 2006

Brownell, B., ed., *Transmaterial 2: A Catalog of Materials that Redefine our Physical Environment,* Princeton Architectural Press, New York, 2008

Evans, R., *Translations from Drawing to Building and Other Essays*, Architectural Association, London, 1997

Farrelly, L., *Representational Techniques*, AVA, Lausanne, 2008

Fiell, C. and Fiell, P., eds, *Designing the 21st Century*, Taschen, Cologne, 2005

Garcia, M., *Patterns of Architecture*, Architectural Design, vol. 79, no. 6, John Wiley & Sons, London, 2009

Gibson J., *The Senses Considered as Perceptual Systems*, Houghton Mifflin, Boston, 1996

Halliday, S., *Green Guide to the Architect's Job Book*, second edition, RIBA Publishing, London, 2007

Holl, S., *Questions of Perception: Phenomenology of Architecture*, a + u Publishing, Tokyo, 1994

Hornung, D., *Colour: A Workshop for Artists and Designers*, Laurence King, London, 2005

Hudson, J., *Process: 50 Product Designs from Concept to Manufacture*, Laurence King, London, 2008

Iwamoto, L., *Digital Fabrications: Architectural and Material Techniques,* Princeton Architectural Press, New York, 2009

Itten, J., *The Elements of Color: A Treatise on the Color System of Johannes Itten Based on his Book The Art of Color,* John Wiley & Sons, 1970

Kawashima, K., *Art Textiles of the World: Japan*, Telos, Brighton, 1997

Kolarevic, B., *Architecture in the Digital Age: Design and Manufacturing*, Taylor & Francis, London, 2005

Kolarevic, B., *Manufacturing Material Effects: Rethinking Design and Making in Architecture,* Routledge, London, 2008

Lawson, B., *How Designers Think*, fourth edition, Architectural Press, Oxord, 2009

Lefteri, C., *Materials for Inspirational Design*, Rotovision, Brighton, 2006

Littlefield, D., and Lewis, S., *Architectural Voices: Listening to Old Buildings,* John Wiley & Sons, Chichester, 2007

Massey, A., *Interior Design Since 1900*, Thames & Hudson, London, 2008

Meerwein, G., Rodeck, B., and Mahnke, F. H., *Color: Communication in Architectural Space*, Birkhäuser, Basel, 2007

Pallasmaa, J., *The Eyes of the Skin: Architecture and the Senses*, John Wiley & Sons, Chichester, 2005

Pallasmaa, J., *The Thinking Hand*, John Wiley & Sons, Chichester, 2009

Pile, J., *A History of Interior Design*, Laurence King, London, 2000

Quinn, B., *The Fashion of Architecture*, Berg, Oxford, 2003

Ritter, A., *Smart Materials in Architecture, Interior Architecture and Design: Types, Products, Architecture*, Birkhäuser, Basel, 2006

Schröpfer, T., *Material Design: Informing Architecture by Materiality*, Birkhäuser, Basel, 2010

Scott, F., *On Altering Architecture*, Routledge, London and New York, 2008

Spankie, R., *Drawing out the Interior*, AVA, Lausanne, 2009

Sparke, P., *The Modern Interior*, Reaktion, London, 2008

Taylor, M., and Preston, J., eds, *Intimus: Interior Design Theory Reader*, John Wiley & Sons, Chichester, 2006

The Building Regulations 2000: Materials and Workmanship, Approved Document to Support Regulation 7, Stationery Office, London, 2006

Thomas, K. L., *Material Matters: Architecture and Material Practice*, Taylor & Francis, London and New York, 2009

Thompson, R., *Manufacturing Processes for Design Professionals*, Thames & Hudson, London, 2007

Ursprung, P., ed., *Herzog & de Meuron, Natural History*, Canadian Centre for Architecture and Lars Müller Publishers, Zurich, 2002

Zumthor, P., *Atmospheres*, Birkhäuser, Basel, 2006

Useful websites

Azom, The A to Z of Materials
www.azom.com

Connect, Materials Knowledge Transfer Network
https://connect.innovateuk.org/web/materialsktn

Design Museum
www.designmuseum.org

Designboom
www.designboom.com

Design inSite
www.designinsite.dk

dezeen
www.dezeen.com

Forest Stewardship Council
www.fsc.org

Frame, Mark and Elephant (online journals)
www.frameweb.com

Materia
http://www.materia.nl/

Material ConneXion
http://www.materialconnexion.com

Material Lab
http://www.material-lab.co.uk

matériO
http://www.materio.com/

Tate
www.tate.org.uk

Transstudio
www.transstudio.com

USGBC, The United States Green Building Council
http://www.usgbc.org/

University of Texas at Austin School of Architecture Materials Lab
http://soa.utexas.edu/matlab/

Index

Picture credits

T = top, L = left, R = right, C = center, B = bottom

Front cover softwall + softblock modular system, molo design, ltd.
Back cover Litracon Kft, Hungary, www.litracon.hu
1 David Joseph: 3 ©Paul Tahon and Ronan and Erwan Bouroullec; 6 ©Studio Bouroullec; 7 Rachael Brown; 8L Vassilis Skopelitis; 8T and BR Rachael Brown; 9T Rachael Brown; 9B Muracciole_Ansorg; 10T ©OMA/DACS 2012; 10B Robin Walker; 11 (except TC) ©2004–2010 Mayang Adnin and William Smith, www.mayang.com/textures; 11TC Shell Shock Designs Ltd; 12 courtesy of Zaha Hadid Architects; 14 ©Ronan Bouroullec; 15 Mary Stevenson Cassatt, American, 1844–1926, *The Tea*, about 1880, oil on canvas, 64.77 x 92.07cm (25½ x 36½ in.), Museum of Fine Arts, Boston, M. Theresa B. Hopkins Fund, 42.178; 16L William Morris Gallery, London Borough of Waltham Forest; 16R ©Sandy Young, Alamy; 17T ©Paul M.R. Maeyaert/©DACS 2012; 17B ©Paul M.R. Maeyaert; 18TL photo: Secession; 18BL courtesy Philippe Garner; 18R The Stapleton Collection, interior with furniture designed by Ruhlmann, from a collection of prints published in four volumes by Albert Levy, c.1924–26 (pochoir print); 19T Jordi Sarrà; 19B Frank den Oudsten/©DACS 2012; 20L Briony Whitmarsh/©DACS 2012 ; 20R Roger Tyrell/©FLC/ADAGP Paris, and DACS, London 2012; 21L photo: Ian Tilton, www.iantilton.net; 21R ©Victoria and Albert Museum; 22 ©OMA/DACS 2012; 23T ©Richard Glover/VIEW; 23L ©Andreas von Einsiedel/Alamy; 23R Comme des Garçons, New York, courtesy AL_A. Commissioned and completed as Future Systems; 24 ©Paul Tahon and Ronan and Erwan Bouroullec; 25 courtesy Thonet; 26 Rachael Brown; 27L courtesy of Zaha Hadid Architects; 27C Ushida Findlay Architects; 27R Litracon Kft, Hungary, www.litracon.hu; 28 photo: Frank Hanswijk, Studio Rolf.fr (www.rolf.fr) in partnership with Zecc Architecten (www.zecc.nl); 30 Rachael Brown; 31 Dalziel and Pow Design Consultants; 33 photos: Frank Hanswijk, Studio Rolf.fr (www.rolf.fr) in partnership with Zecc Architecten (www.zecc.nl); 34T Dow Jones Architects; 34B David Grandorge; 35 Louise Melchior; 36–37 photos: Rachael Brown and Lorraine Farrelly, artworks: Rachael Ball; 38–39 photos: Rachael Brown, artworks: Rachael Ball, Alja Petrauskaite, Amber Hurdy, Maxine Tamakloe, Alexandra Gheorghian; 40 David Barbour/BDP; 41 Rachael Brown; 42L Belinda Mitchell; 42R Rachael Brown; 43 ©The Estate of Eva Hesse/courtesy Hauser & Wirth; 44 ©Reuters/Corbis; 45 Rachael Brown; 46TL and R Tactility Factory Ltd; 46CL Hazel Hewitt; 46CR, BL and R Teresa Dietrich Photography, www.teresadietrich.com; 47 photos: Rachael Brown, artworks: Rachael Ball; 48–49 photos: Rachael Brown, artworks: Kate McDermott, Claire Magri-Overend, Viviana Diaz, Emma Curtis; 50TL photo: James Waddel; 50TR courtesy Junko Mori; 50BL courtesy David Leefe Kendon; 50BR courtesy Will Spankie, www.willspankie.com; 51 photos: Rachael Brown; 52 Rogier Jaarsma, www.rogierjaarsma.nl; 54TL and B Rocket Mattler and Kyle Ford; 54TR Gabrielle Coffey; 56 photos: Mag. Eveline Tilley-Tietze and Stuart A. Veech; client: D. Swarovski & Co; project: Swarovski trade show stand at the BASELWORLD Watch and Jewellery Fair 2008, Basel; project time frame: all stages of concept, design and realization – 11 weeks; design team VMA: Stuart A. Veech, Mascha Veech-Kosmatschof, Peter Mitterer, Ange Weppernig; project and site supervision: VMA, werkraum wien ingenieure; animated graphics: Neville Brody/Research Studios, London; lighting concept: Stuart A. Veech; consulting HVAC: TGA Consulting GmbH; general contractor: Veech Media Architecure GmbH (VMA); subcontractors: Gahrens + Battermann, Deko Trend KEG; 57 Fiona Brocklesby; 58L Sanna Fischer-Payne/BDP; 58R Lorraine Farrelly; 60 Paul Warchol; 61 ©Studio Bouroullec and V&A Images, Victoria and Albert Museum; 62 photo: Christopher Burke, artist: Sarah Morris, image courtesy of Friedrich Petzel Gallery, New York; 63 ©Richard Glover/VIEW; 64 Åke E:son Lindman; 65 David Joseph; 66 Chris Bosse, Peter Murphy; 67TL Hampshire County Council Property Services, interior design with artist Eileen White; 67R Hampshire County Council Property Services; 67BL David Barbour/BDP; 69T Lorraine Farrelly; 69BL and R Rachael Brown; 70T Roger Tyrell; 70B Ralph Kamena; 71 ©Eduard Hueber/archphoto.com; 72T Ben Cole; 72B Rachael Brown and Lorraine Farrelly; 73T Marcel Wanders; 73B Cole and Son; 74T photo: Rachael Brown, artwork: Munerah Almedeiheem; 74B: Rachael Brown; 75 Rachael Brown; 76T Roger Tyrell; 76B Nicola Crowson; 77T and C Noboru Kawaghishi; 77B HATTA; 78 Fiona Damiano; 80 Joke Brouwer; 81 Rachael Ball and Lorraine Farrelly, based on Desso Carpets' diagram; 82L Louis Basquiast; 82R Winter/Hörbelt/©DACS 2012 ; 84TL Eek en Ruigrok; 84TR Gerard van Hees; 84B All rights reserved ©2011 David Watson and Stig Evans; 85T photo: Toshihide Kajiwara, Design Spirits Co. Ltd, Interior Designer: Yuhkichi Kawai; Lighting Designer: Muse_D Inc., Kazuhiko Suzuki & Misuzu Yagi; 85B Rachael Brown and Lorraine Farrelly; 86 Debbie Riddle 2010; 87TL and C Eek en Ruigrok; 87TR David Cripps; 87 bottom three images Rogier Jaarsma, www.rogierjaarsma.nl; 89TL and C Roger Tyrell; 89TR Lorraine Farrelly; 89B Alan Matlock;

90T Alan Matlock; 90B ©Tetsuya Ito; 91 ©Richard Bryant/Arcaid; 92–93 Rachael Brown; 94 Andrew Kudless; 95 photos: Christof Gaggl; Technicolor Bloom credits: Brennan Buck, Freeland Buck with Rob Henderson, Dumene Comploi, Elizabeth Brauner, Eva Diem, Manfred Herman, Maja Ozvaldic, Anna Psenicka, Bika Rebeck; 96T ©Ronan and Erwan Bouroullec; 96B ©Paul Tahon and Ronan and Erwan Bouroullec; 97T ©Paul Tahon and Ronan and Erwan Bouroullec; 97B Glenn Norwood; 98 Phil Meech/©OMA/DACS 2012 ; 99 photos: Rachael Brown, artworks: Rachael Ball, Alexandra Gheorghian; 100CR Rachael Ball, all other images Rachael Brown ; 101 top six images Rachael Ball; 101 bottom three images Rachael Brown; 102–103 Rachael Brown and Lorraine Farrelly; 104–105 Rachael Brown; 106 Ushida Findlay Architects; 108 Fiona Damiano; 109 Anne-Laure Carruth in collaboration with Joanna Lewis; 110 top two rows Rachael Brown; 110 bottom two rows photos: Belinda Mitchell, artworks: Jekaterina Zlotnikova, Erin Hunter, Krishna Mistry; 111 Fiona Damiano; 112L Sarah Sze; 112R photo: Tom Powel Imaging, artwork: Jessica Stockholder, courtesy P.S.1 Contemporary Art Center; 113 left column Michael Bates; 113 right column Rachael Brown; 114TL photo: Belinda Mitchell, artwork: Kendal James; 114BL photo: Nicola Crowson, artwork: Jonathan Adegbenro; 114BR photo: Belinda Mitchell, artwork: Christina Kanari; 115 Paul Cashin and Simon Drayson; 116–117 Rachael Brown; 118–119 Rachael Brown and Lorraine Farrelly; 120T Rachael Brown; 120B photo: Rachael Brown, model: Steven Palanee; 121T Steven Palanee; 121B Rachael Brown; 122L photo: Belinda Mitchell, artwork: Katie Horton and Stacey Close; 122R Rachael Brown; 123T photo: Rachael Brown, model: Jonathan Adegbenro; 123TR photo: Rachael Brown, model: Dan Terry, Rob Kahn, Jonny Sage; 123BL photo: Rachael Brown, model: Khalid Saleh; 123BR photo: Rachael Brown, artwork: Amy Farn; 124T Iwona Galazka; 124BL and R Cinimod Studios; 125 Sajeeda Panjwani; 126 Ushida Findlay Architects; 127T Robin Walker; 127B Tony Tan; 128 Fiona Damiano; 129 photos: Rachael Brown, presentations, clockwise from TL: Jekaterina Zlotnikova, Zina Ghanawi, Fiona Damiano; 130–131 photos: Rachael Brown, artworks: Natalie Bernasconi; 132–133 Fiona Damiano; 134 Rachael Brown and Lorraine Farrelly; 135 Kvadrat; 136T Peterfotograph/Offecct, Soundwave®Flo; 136B Fritz Hansen; 138 Pawel Korab Kowalski/Puff-Buff; 140 Materia Inspiration Centre; 142–143 metal panelling, metal, wood, stone and flooring ©2004–2010, Mayang Adnin and William Smith, www.mayang.com/textures; all other images Rachael Brown and Lorraine Farrelly; 144L ©2004–2010, Mayang Adnin and William Smith, www.mayang.com/textures; 144R Lauren Moriarty; 145 top row Rachael Brown and Lorraine Farrelly; 145C Ralph Kamena; 145BL Radek Achramowicz/Puff-Buff; 145BR Pawel Korab Kowalski/Puff-Buff; 146TL, TR, BL Rachael Brown and Lorraine Farrelly; 146BR ©2004–2010, Mayang Adnin and William Smith, www.mayang.com/textures; 147T Paul Warchol; 147B Ralph Kamena; 148L Toshihide Kajiwara; 148TC Rachael Brown; 148TR and BC Rachael Brown and Lorraine Farrelly; 148CL and R ©2004–2010, Mayang Adnin and William Smith, www.mayang.com/textures; 148BR Bamboo Flooring Company, www.bambooflooringcompany.com; 149TL and TR Rachael Brown; 149TC Cole and Son; 149BL Vassilis Skopelitis; 149C and BR ©2004–2010, Mayang Adnin and William Smith, www.mayang.com/textures; 150T ©Studio Fred & Fred; architect: Studio 54; project: Exhibition EURATECHNOLOGIE, Lille, France; 150C Levi's; 150BL and C ©2004–2010, Mayang Adnin and William Smith, www.mayang.com/textures; 150BR Rachael Brown; 151 ©2004–2010, Mayang Adnin and William Smith, www.mayang.com/textures; 152 top row ©2004–2010, Mayang Adnin and William Smith, www.mayang.com/textures; 152BL Shell Shock Designs, Ltd, www.shellshockdesigns.com; 152BR Zoubida Tulkens; 153T and CL ©2004–2010, Mayang Adnin and William Smith, www.mayang.com/textures; all other images Rachael Brown; 155 ©Gramazio & Kohler, ETH Zürich; 156TL 100% Design; 156BL and R Rachael Brown; 158TL ©matériO; 158TR Materia Inspiration Centre; 158B Matthew Stansfield/Material Lab/Boomerang PR Ltd; 159L Rachael Brown; 159R ©100% Design; 160 Nicolas Borel; 162 Barry Johnson; 163 Design Spirits Co. Ltd; 164–165 Jump Studios; 166 TN29; 167L photo: Uli Schade; footwear: Tracey Neuls; sculpture: Nina Saunders; textiles: Sanderson's; 167R Nicola Yeoman and Tracey Neuls; 168–169L and B Matthias Givell – Bonniers Konsthall, Stockholm, Sweden, courtesy Gunilla Klingberg and Galerie Nordenhake/©DACS 2012; 169TR Peter Geschwind, courtesy Gunilla Klingberg and Galerie Nordenhake/©DACS 2012; 170–173 molo design, ltd.; 174–175 Alex Hoare, Lybster, June 2010; 174TC Waterlines Museum, Lybster; 176–177 photos: John Maclean for Casson Mann; lead exhibition design: Casson Mann; graphic design: Nick Bell; interactive exhibition strategy: All of Us; lighting: dha design; 178 Nicolas Borel; 179 Jakob + MacFarlane; 180 Sanna Fisher-Payne/BDP; 181 photos: Stephen Anderson, drawings: BDP and TinTab; 183T ©Peter Cook/VIEW; 183B ©Hufton + Crow/VIEW

Authors' acknowledgments

This book has only been possible because so many people have been prepared to give their time to discuss ideas and provide information for its publication. We have enjoyed the collaboration and we are most grateful.

Special thanks go to Belinda Mitchell, Senior Lecturer at Portsmouth University, for the many helpful discussions when we began this book, and particularly her contributions regarding the sensory properties of materials and communicating material thinking (some of Belinda's comments were informed by *The Sensory Experience of Space* (2008), a research project led by Belinda Mitchell and Kate Baker. Artists, dancers, and scenographers were also involved). Thanks also go to Clare Qualmann, artist, lecturer, and materials librarian, for her inspiring thoughts and words about artists and their materials and material classifications; and to Matt Sheard, designer and historian, particularly for his thoughts regarding the history of materials.

Thanks go to the following Portsmouth students: David Holden, for his photography; to research assistant Amy Walker, who has been very patient and meticulous in her support of the authors; and to Rachael Ball and Fiona Damiano, whose projects and drawings feature in the book. We would also like to give our thanks to the many other students at the University of Portsmouth's School of Architecture who are featured or who have taken part in projects and exercises that have supported the content of the book; we are very sorry that we cannot name you all.

In addition, our sincere thanks go to the numerous practitioners who have contributed so generously to this publication, particularly Ben Kelly of Ben Kelly Design, Kevin Brennan of Brinkworth, and Simon Jackson of Jump Studios, who all gave time to discuss their approach to using materials in the interior. All of the practitioners who are included in this book have been incredibly supportive and have supplied information about their design projects that have inspired the authors—and, we hope, the designers of the future.

Finally, we must acknowledge the support of the editorial team at Laurence King: thanks to Philip Cooper for encouraging the development of the book, Liz Faber for her support and direction as editor, production controller Srijana Gurung, and designer John Round.